Declaration on the Way

Declaration on the Way

Church, Ministry, and Eucharist

Committee on Ecumenical
and Interreligious Affairs,
United States Conference of Catholic Bishops

Evangelical Lutheran Church in America

Augsburg Fortress
Minneapolis

DECLARATION ON THE WAY
Church, Ministry, and Eucharist

Cover art: The Road to Emmaus by He Qi (www.heqiart.com)
Cover design: Laurie Ingram
Book design: PerfecType, Nashville, TN

Print ISBN: 978-1-5064-1616-8
eBook ISBN: 978-1-5064-1617-5

The paper used in this publication meets the minimum requirements of American National Standard for Information Sciences—Permanence of Paper for Printed Library Materials, ANSI Z329.48-1984.

Manufactured in the USA
20 19 18 17 16   3 4 5 6 7 8 9 10

Contents

The document *Declaration on the Way: Church, Ministry, and Eucharist* was developed as a resource by the Committee on Ecumenical and Interreligious Affairs of the United States Conference of Catholic Bishops (USCCB) and Ecumenical and Inter-Religious Relations in the Office of the Presiding Bishop of the Evangelical Lutheran Church in America (ELCA).

It was authorized by the committee chairman, Bishop Mitchell T. Rozanski. It has been directed for publication by the undersigned.

Msgr. Ronny E. Jenkins, JCD
General Secretary, USCCB

It was reviewed by Presiding Bishop Elizabeth A. Eaton of the ELCA and has been authorized for publication by the undersigned.

The Rev. Wm Chris Boerger
Secretary, ELCA

Members of the Task Force

Catholics

Cochair:
Bishop Denis J. Madden,
Auxiliary Bishop of Baltimore, Maryland

Rev. Dr. Brian E. Daley, SJ
University of Notre Dame, South Bend, Indiana

Rev. Dr. Jared Wicks, SJ
Pontifical College Josephinum, Columbus, Ohio

Dr. Susan K. Wood, SCL
Marquette University, Milwaukee, Wisconsin

Staff:
Rev. John W. Crossin, OSFS
United States Conference of Catholic Bishops, Washington, D.C.

Lutherans

Cochair:
Rev. Mark S. Hanson
*Presiding Bishop Emeritus, Evangelical Lutheran Church in America;
Augsburg College, Minneapolis, Minnesota*

Dr. Kathryn L. Johnson
Louisville Presbyterian Theological Seminary, Louisville, Kentucky

Rev. Dr. William G. Rusch
(initial meetings)
Yale University, New Haven, Connecticut

Rev. Dr. Joy A. Schroeder
Capital University/Trinity Lutheran Seminary, Columbus, Ohio

Staff:

Rev. Donald J. McCoid
Evangelical Lutheran Church in America, Chicago, Illinois

Dialogues Consulted and Abbreviations

The members of the *Declaration on the Way* task force offer grati-
tude to all who have participated in Catholic–Lutheran dialogues
during the last five decades and acknowledge their profound
dependence on the work accomplished in these international
and regional (national and local) dialogues. This *Declaration* has
especially drawn from the following dialogue reports, which are
available in online as well as published versions.

International dialogues and studies

*Report of the Joint Lutheran–Roman Catholic Study Commission on
"The Gospel and the Church"* (1972). Cited as *Malta Report.*

Das Herrenmahl/The Eucharist (1978). Lutheran/Roman Catholic
Joint Commission. Frankfurt am Main: Verlag Bonifatius-
Druckerei Paderborn/Otto Lembeck, 1978; Geneva: The
Lutheran World Federation, 1980. Cited as *The Eucharist.*

All Under One Christ (1980). Roman Catholic/Lutheran Joint
Commission Statement on the Augsburg Confession.

The Ministry in the Church (1981). Roman Catholic/Lutheran
Joint Commission. Geneva: The Lutheran World Federation, 1982. Cited as *Ministry.*

Kirche und Rechtfertigung/Church and Justification (1993). Lutheran–Roman Catholic Joint Commission. Frankfurt am Main: Verlag Bonifatius-Druckerei Paderborn/Otto Lembeck, 1994; Geneva: The Lutheran World Federation, 1994. Cited as *Church and Justification*.

The Apostolicity of the Church: Study Document of the Lutheran–Roman Catholic Commission on Unity (2006). Minneapolis: Lutheran University Press, 2006. Cited as *Apostolicity*.

From Conflict to Communion. Lutheran–Catholic Common Commemoration of the Reformation in 2017 (2013). Report of the Lutheran–Roman Catholic Commission on Unity. Leipzig: Evangelische Verlagsanstalt and Paderborn: Bonifatius, 2013. Cited as *From Conflict to Communion*.

Regional and national dialogues and studies

The Eucharist as Sacrifice: Lutherans and Catholics in Dialogue III (1967). Washington, D.C.: Bishops' Committee for Ecumenical and Interreligious Affairs; New York: U.S.A. National Committee for The Lutheran World Federation, 1967. Cited as *Eucharist as Sacrifice*.

Eucharist and Ministry: Lutherans and Catholics in Dialogue IV (1970). Washington, D.C.: Bishops' Committee for Ecumenical and Interreligious Affairs; New York: U.S.A. National Committee for The Lutheran World Federation, 1970. Cited as *Eucharist and Ministry*.

Teaching Authority and Infallibility in the Church: Lutherans and Catholics in Dialogue VI, eds. Paul C. Empie, T. Austin Murphy, and Joseph A. Burgess. Minneapolis: Augsburg, 1978.

Kirchengemeinschaft in Wort und Sakrament (1984). Bilateral Working Group of the German National Bishops' Conference and the Church Leadership of the United Evangelical Lutheran Church of Germany. Paderborn: Bonifatius, 1984.

Communio Sanctorum: The Church as the Communion of Saints (2000). Bilateral Working Group of the German National Bishops' Conference and the Church Leadership of the United Evangelical Lutheran Church of Germany. English translation by Mark W. Jeske, Michael Root, and Daniel R. Smith. Collegeville: 2004. Cited as *Communio Sanctorum*.

The Church as Koinonia of Salvation: Its Structures and Ministries (2004). Bishops' Committee for Ecumenical and Inter-religious Affairs, United States Conference of Catholic Bishops; Department for Ecumenical Affairs, Evangelical Lutheran Church in America; edited by Randall Lee, Jeffrey Gross. Washington, D.C.: United States Conference of Catholic Bishops, 2005. Cited as *Church as Koinonia of Salvation*.

Justification in the Life of the Church: A Report from the Roman Catholic–Lutheran Dialogue Group for Sweden and Finland (2010). English translation by Sr. Gerd Swenson. Uppsala, Stockholm, and Helsinki: Church of Sweden, Roman-Catholic Diocese of Stockholm, Evangelical-Lutheran Church of Finland, Roman-Catholic Diocese of Helsinki, 2010. Cited as *Justification in the Life of the Church*.

Hope of Eternal Life: Lutherans and Catholics in Dialogue XI (2011). Edited by Lowell G. Almen and Richard J. Sklba. Minneapolis: Lutheran University Press, 2011. Cited as *Hope of Eternal Life*.

Abbreviations

AG	*Ad Gentes*. Decree on the Missionary Activity of the Church. Second Vatican Council.
BC	*The Book of Concord: The Confessions of the Evangelical Lutheran Church*, eds. Robert Kolb and Timothy J. Wengert. Minneapolis: Fortress Press, 2000.
BEM	*Baptism, Eucharist, and Ministry*. Faith and Order Paper 111. Geneva: World Council of Churches, 1982.
CA	Augsburg Confession, 1530, in *The Book of Concord*.
CD	*Christus Dominus*. Decree on the Pastoral Office of Bishops in the Church. Second Vatican Council.
DH	*Henrich Denzinger Compendium of Creeds, Definitions, and Declarations on Matters of Faith and Morals*, revised, enlarged, and in collaboration with Helmut Hoping, edited by Peter Hünermann for the original bilingual edition and edited by Robert Fastiggi and Anne Englund Nash for the English Edition, 43rd Edition. San Francisco: Ignatius Press, 2012.
DS	*Enchiridion symbolorum, definitionum, et declarationum de rebus fidei et morum*, Henricus Denzinger et Adolphus Schönmetzer, ed. XXXIII. Herder: Barcinone, Friburgi Brisgoviae, et alibi, 1965. References by paragraph number.
DV	*Dei Verbum*. Dogmatic Constitution on Divine Revelation. Second Vatican Council.

JDDJ   *Joint Declaration on the Doctrine of Justification* (1999) by The Lutheran World Federation and the Roman Catholic Church.

LG   *Lumen Gentium.* Dogmatic Constitution on the Church. Second Vatican Council.

Lund Statement   *Episcopal Ministry within the Apostolicity of the Church* (2007). The Lutheran World Federation, 2008.

LW   *Luther's Works.* Published in 55 volumes by Concordia Publishing House and Fortress Press, St. Louis and Philadelphia, 1958–86.

LWF   The Lutheran World Federation

PCPCU   Pontifical Council for Promoting Christian Unity

PO   *Presbyterorum Ordinis.* Decree on the Ministry and Life of Priests. Second Vatican Council.

Tanner   *Decrees of the Ecumenical Councils,* Norman P. Tanner, SJ, ed. London/Washington: Sheed and Ward/Georgetown University Press, 1990.

UR   *Unitatis Redintegratio.* Decree on Ecumenism. Second Vatican Council.

VELKD   Vereinigte Evangelisch-Lutherische Kirche Deutschlands (United Evangelical Lutheran Church of Germany).

WA   "Weimar Ausgabe": *D. Martin Luthers Werke, Kritische Gesamtausgabe,* Hermann Böhlhaus Nachfolger, Weimar, Germany.

WCC   World Council of Churches

Preface

This document, *Declaration on the Way: Church, Ministry, and Eucharist*, is a declaration of the consensus achieved by Lutherans and Catholics on the topics of church, ministry, and eucharist as the result of ecumenical dialogue between the two communions since 1965. It is a consensus "on the way" (*in via*), because dialogue has not yet resolved all the church-dividing differences on these topics. Nevertheless, at this time of important benchmarks in the relationship between Lutherans and Catholics, including both the anniversary of 50 years of dialogue in 2015 and also the 500th commemoration of the Reformation in 2017, it is good to review the path traveled together and to enumerate the many points of agreement between Lutherans and Catholics on these subjects. This review can help both communities to affirm the agreements they have reached together. More importantly, it can encourage them to look for the next steps toward Christian unity.

The document consists of an introduction, a "Statement of Agreements" followed by "Agreements in the Lutheran–Roman Catholic Dialogues—Elaborated and Documented," a section titled "Remaining Differences and Reconciling Considerations," and a conclusion. The "Statement of Agreements" consists of consensus statements on the topics of church, ministry, and eucharist that Catholics and Lutherans affirm together.

The section "Agreements in the Lutheran–Roman Catholic Dialogues—Elaborated and Documented" is correlated with the preceding "Statement of Agreements" so that each numbered agreement corresponds with the number in the following section that documents and elaborates on that particular agreement. This section gives references to specific dialogue statements that provide the basis for the agreements in the preceding section.

The section "Remaining Differences and Reconciling Considerations" is not directly correlated to the preceding sections but enumerates a number of topics that have traditionally divided Lutherans and Catholics regarding church, ministry, and eucharist. Each topic is developed in three parts. The first part, which appears in italics, states the controverted issue between Catholics and Lutherans. The second part develops reconciling considerations that contribute to mitigating or resolving the difference. The third part provides possible resolutions or steps forward. In some instances, the difference is determined to be no longer church-dividing, and the document calls for a recognition of this fact by our ecclesial bodies. For other topics, the document recommends further study, clarification, and dialogue.

The hope in offering this *Declaration* is that the Lutheran and Catholic communions at all levels will receive and affirm the consensus statements in the section "Statement of Agreements" as the achievement of our ecumenical dialogues on both the international and regional levels since their inception in 1965. The *Declaration* also offers encouragement that together Catholics and Lutherans will find ways to move forward where work remains to be done.

I. Introduction

"I think then that the one goal of all who are really and truly serving the Lord ought to be to bring back to union the churches which have at different times and in diverse manners divided from one another."

ST. BASIL THE GREAT (330–379), "EPISTLE CXIV"

As Catholics and Lutherans, we have not yet achieved the goal of unity that is God's gift in Christ and to which St. Basil calls us. Yet we have come a long distance from the disunity, suspicions, and even hostilities that characterized our relationships for generations. This *Declaration on the Way (In Via)* to unity seeks to make more visible the unity we share by gathering together agreements reached on issues of church, ministry, and eucharist. This *Declaration*, a distinctive kind of ecumenical text, is "on the way" because it is neither at the beginning nor the end of the journey toward unity. It identifies

32 statements where Lutherans and Catholics have consensus on matters regarding church, ministry, and eucharist, while recognizing also that not all differences on these doctrines have been reconciled at this time.

This *Declaration on the Way* is not the result of another dialogue on these topics nor yet a declaration of full consensus on them. Rather, it harvests the results of 50 years of international and regional dialogues in the belief that now is the time to claim the unity achieved through these agreements, to establish church practices that reflect this growth into communion, and to commit ourselves anew to taking the next steps forward.

The doctrines of church, ministry, and eucharist suggest themselves for this *Declaration* for two principal reasons. Clearly, our differences concerning these doctrines are among the most significant issues we must address in order for us to grow in our real but imperfect communion. Moreover, the three issues are inseparably intertwined with one another. While there is already substantial agreement concerning the eucharist itself, full eucharistic communion depends also upon the mutual recognition of ministry, which is in turn dependent upon the recognition of each ecclesial community as truly apostolic. Thus, the teaching of both Catholics and Lutherans that recognizes imperfect communion between them supports a partial but real recognition of ministry.

This *Declaration* demonstrates that cumulatively the global and regional Lutheran–Catholic dialogues have made significant progress in resolving our differences on these three core doctrines. Therefore, drawing upon the results of these dialogues, this *Declaration* commends 32 agreements on church, ministry, and eucharist for ecclesial recognition, and supplies supporting documentation for these agreements from ecumenical dialogues. Further, without any pretensions of being exhaustive, it identifies remaining differences and sketches some possible ways forward. Reception of the "Statement of Agreements" by the appropriate bodies of The Lutheran World Federation and the Catholic Church with a corresponding commitment to address the remaining questions will move us significantly forward on the way to full communion.

Inspirations and Aspirations

The inspirations and aspirations behind this *Declaration on the Way* are many. An important one is the December 2011 speech given by Cardinal Kurt Koch, president of the Pontifical Council for Promoting Christian Unity. Seeking the next steps beyond the work of *Harvesting the Fruits* presented by Cardinal Walter Kasper in 2009,[1] he noted the need to identify and receive the achievements of bilateral dialogues and to indicate ways forward for resolving remaining differences.

Another significant inspiration is the 2012 document of the international Lutheran–Roman Catholic Commission on Unity, *From Conflict to Communion: Lutheran–Catholic Commemoration of the Reformation in 2017*. This *Declaration on the Way* responds to two of the "ecumenical imperatives" with which the report concludes:

> 1. Catholics and Lutherans should always begin from the perspective of unity and not from the point of view of division in order to strengthen what is held in common even though the differences are more easily seen and experienced.

---

1. Cardinal Walter Kasper, *Harvesting the Fruits: Basic Aspects of Christian Faith in Ecumenical Dialogue* (London/New York: Continuum, 2009).

2. Lutherans and Catholics must let themselves continuously be transformed by the encounter with each other and by mutual witness of faith.

The leadership of Pope Francis, who has frequently stressed the importance of ecumenism for the church's mission, also inspires this *Declaration*. In *Evangelii Gaudium*, he declared:

> The credibility of the Christian message would be much greater if Christians could overcome their divisions and the Church could realize "the fullness of catholicity proper to her in those of her children who, though joined to her by baptism, are yet separated from full communion with her." We must never forget that we are pilgrims journeying alongside one another. This means that we must have sincere trust in our fellow pilgrims, putting aside all suspicion or mistrust, and turn our gaze to what we are all seeking: the radiant peace of God's face.[2]

Why Now?

Why now? Because among the faithful there is a "holy impatience" as they pray and long for clearer and deeper expressions of our unity in Christ. As The Lutheran World Federation General Secretary Martin Junge has said, the baptized are not only accountable to God for living out the unity given to them but accountable also to one another, "particularly to those who bear the costs of Christian separation."[3] Thus, ecumenical work must

---

2. Pope Francis, Apostolic Exhortation, *Evangelii Gaudium*, 24 November 2013, §244, citing the Second Vatican Council, *Unitatis Redintegratio*, 4.

3. Martin Junge, "In Pursuing Christian Unity We Have a Double Accountability," *Lutheran World Information* 11/2011, 3. He mentioned in particular "where Christian families cannot be nourished together at the Lord's Table because church leaders are not yet able to resolve theological differences; where Christians must explain in interfaith contexts why they cannot worship

hold itself responsible not only for its "theological honesty, rigor and quest for truth but also for its urgency and its love."

Why now? Because when political and religious contexts are so often experienced as polarized, fragmented, and fearful of differences at all levels, we have the opportunity to witness the good news that "if anyone is in Christ, there is a new creation: everything old has passed away: see, everything has become new! All this is from God, who reconciled us to himself through Christ, and has given us the ministry of reconciliation" (2 Corinthians 5:17–18).

Why now? Because through 50 years of theological dialogues, Catholics and Lutherans have shown repeatedly that we have the resolve and the capacity to address doctrines and practices that have kept us apart. Through our dialogues, we are renewed in our commitment to continue together on the way to full communion, when we will experience our unity in sharing the eucharist, in the full recognition of each other's ministries and of our being Christ's church.

An outstanding fruit of these dialogues was the *Joint Declaration on the Doctrine of Justification*. Here Catholics and Lutherans demonstrated how, through sustained theological dialogues and prayer, a major doctrine once deemed to be church-dividing can become a teaching in which we find our unity through reconciled diversity. The *JDDJ* provided an ecumenical breakthrough in distinguishing divisive mutual condemnations from diversities in theology and piety which need not divide the church, but which can in fact enrich it. Thus, the *JDDJ* inspires our two communions to continue further on

under one roof; where coordinated diaconal response to the needs of the world is undercut by our feuding; where gifts of one part of Christ's Body are withheld or denied in other parts because we have built walls of separation."

this road in relation to other issues inhibiting further growth in communion.

Why now? Because in 2017 we will commemorate the 500th anniversary of a reformation movement that began in deep divisions and now calls us to the continued work of reconciliation for the sake of the gospel and our witness and work in the world.

Responding to the convergence of these considerations, the leadership of the Evangelical Lutheran Church in America and the Bishops' Committee for Ecumenical and Interreligious Affairs of the United States Conference of Catholic Bishops convened a theological task force in 2012 to develop this *Declaration on the Way* on the themes of church, ministry, and eucharist.

Reception of the Statements of Agreement

This *Declaration on the Way* is presented with the prayer that it be affirmed and received into our common life. It is hoped that Catholics and Lutherans at the highest level will receive formally the 32 statements of agreement it contains. It is recommended that together The Lutheran World Federation and the Pontifical Council for Promoting Christian Unity create a process to implement the *Declaration* of these agreements, confirming that there are no longer church-dividing differences with respect to them.

Our journeying together on the way to full communion will also be sustained and renewed when Catholics and Lutherans strengthen their ties of common action at every level, wherever they gather in local communities for prayer, dialogue, and shared service in response to those who live in poverty and on the margins of society.

You are invited to read this *Declaration on the Way* with an open mind and heart as together we seek to discern God's will and to follow it in love.

II. Statement of Agreements

A. Agreements on the Church

The Church's Foundation in God's Saving Work

1 Catholics and Lutherans agree that the church on earth has been assembled by the triune God, who grants to its members their sharing in the triune divine life as God's own people, as the body of the risen Christ, and as the temple of the Holy Spirit, while they are also called to give witness to these gifts so that others may come to share in them.

2 They agree as well that the church on earth arose from the whole event of Jesus Christ, who remains its sole foundation (1 Corinthians 3:11).

3 Further, they hold in common that the church on earth is gathered by the proclamation of the gospel of God's saving mercy in Christ, so that the gospel, proclaimed in the Holy Spirit by the apostles, remains the church's normative origin and abiding foundation.

4 An agreement follows that the church on earth is in every age apostolic, because it is founded upon the apostles' witness to the gospel and it continuously professes the apostolic and evangelical faith while living by mandated practices handed on from the apostles. Thus, Lutherans and Catholics recognize in both their ecclesial communities the attribute of apostolicity grounded in their ongoing continuity in apostolic faith, teaching, and practices.

The Word, Scripture, and Means of Grace

5 Lutherans and Catholics agree that the church on earth lives from and is ruled by the Word of God, which it encounters in Christ, in the living word of the gospel, and in the inspired and canonical Scriptures.

6 They are one in holding that the church on earth participates in Christ's benefits through the historical and perceptible actions of proclaiming the gospel and celebrating the sacraments, as initiated by Christ and handed on by his apostles.

Communion, Visibility, and Hiddenness

7 Catholics and Lutherans agree that the church on earth is a communion (*koinonia*). It shares in God's gifts offered for us by Christ, which, by being held in common, bring believers into unity and fellowship with each other.

8 Consequently, they agree that the church on earth combines audible and visible elements with profound spiritual realities that remain hidden from empirical investigation and perception.

Preservation of the Church and Union with the Saints

9 Catholics and Lutherans agree that the church on earth is indefectible, because it is and will be preserved by the Holy Spirit in all its aspects essential for salvation. They share the certainty of Christian hope that the church, established by Christ and led by his Spirit, will always remain in the truth, fulfilling its mission to humanity for the sake of the gospel.

10 They furthermore agree that the church on earth is united with the community of the saints in glory.

Eschatology and Mission

11 This perspective gives rise to agreement that the church on earth is an anticipatory reality, on pilgrimage and expectant of reaching its final destination in God's ultimate gathering of his people in their entirety when Christ returns and when the Holy Spirit completes the work of sanctification.

12 But Catholics and Lutherans agree as well that the church on earth is mandated to carry out a mission in which it participates in God's activity in the world by evangelization, worship, service of humanity, and care for creation.

B. Agreements on Ordained Ministry

In "Agreements on the Church," Catholics and Lutherans affirm the ecclesial character of one another's communities. This affirmation is an essential first step toward a mutual recognition of ordained ministry, for mutual recognition of one another's ecclesial character is intertwined with the mutual recognition of one another's ministry.

Ministry in the Church

13 Lutherans and Catholics agree that the ordained ministry belongs to the essential elements that express the church's apostolic character and that it also contributes, through the power of the Holy Spirit, to the church's continuing apostolic faithfulness.

14 Catholics and Lutherans agree that all the baptized who believe in Christ share in the priesthood of Christ. For both Catholics and Lutherans, the common priesthood of all the baptized and the special, ordained ministry enhance one another.

Divine Origin of Ministry

15 Lutherans and Catholics affirm together that ordained ministry is of divine origin and that it is necessary for the being of the church. Ministry is not simply a delegation "from below," but is instituted by Jesus Christ.

16 We both affirm that all ministry is subordinated to Christ, who in the Holy Spirit is acting in the preaching of the word of God, in the administration of the sacraments, and in pastoral service.

17 Lutherans and Catholics agree that the proclamation of the gospel is foremost among the various tasks of the ordained ministry.

18 They declare in common that the essential and specific function of the ordained minister is to assemble and build up the Christian community by proclaiming the word of God; celebrating the sacraments; and presiding over the liturgical, missionary, and diaconal life of the community.

Authority of Ministry

19 The authority of the ministry is not to be understood as an individual possession of the minister, but it is rather an authority with the commission to serve in the community and for the community.

20 Catholics and Lutherans also agree that the office of ministry stands over against (*gegenüber*) the community as well as within it and thus is called to exercise authority over the community.

Ordination

21 Catholics and Lutherans agree that entry into this apostolic and God-given ministry is not by baptism but by ordination. They agree that ministers cannot ordain themselves or claim this office as a matter of right but are called by God and designated in and through the church.

22 Catholics and Lutherans both ordain through prayer invoking the Holy Spirit and with the laying on of hands by another ordained person. Both affirm that the ordinand receives an anointing of the Holy Spirit, who equips that person for ordained ministry.

23 Both Lutherans and Catholics regard ordination as unrepeatable.

One Ministerial Office

24 Both consider that there is one ordained ministerial office, while also distinguishing a special ministry of *episkope* over presbyters/pastors.

25 They agree that the ministry is exercised both locally in the congregation and regionally. Both accept that the distinction between local and regional offices in the churches is more than the result of purely historical and human developments, or a matter of sociological necessity, but is the action of the Spirit. Furthermore, the differentiation of the ministry into a more local and a more regional office arises of necessity out of the intention and task of ministry to be a ministry of unity in faith.

Ministry Serving Worldwide Unity

26 Catholics and Lutherans affirm together that all ministry, to the degree that it serves the *koinonia* of salvation, also serves the unity of the worldwide church and that together we long for a more complete realization of this unity.

C. Agreements on the Eucharist

High Esteem for Eucharistic Union with Christ in Holy Communion

27 Lutherans and Catholics agree in esteeming highly the spiritual benefits of union with the risen Christ given to them as they receive his body and blood in Holy Communion.

Trinitarian Dimension of Eucharist

28 Catholics and Lutherans agree that in eucharistic worship the church participates in a unique way in the life of the Trinity: In the power of the Holy Spirit, called down upon the gifts and the worshiping community, believers have access to the glorified flesh and blood of Christ the Son as our food, and are brought in union with him and with each other to the Father.

Eucharist as Reconciling Sacrifice of Christ and as Sacrifice of the Church's Praise and Thanksgiving

29 Catholics and Lutherans agree that eucharistic worship is the memorial (*anamnesis*) of Jesus Christ, present as the one crucified for us and risen, that is, in his sacrificial self-giving for us in his death and in his resurrection (Romans 4:25), to which the church responds with its sacrifice of praise and thanksgiving.

Eucharistic Presence

30 Lutherans and Catholics agree that in the sacrament of the Lord's supper, Jesus Christ himself is present: He is present truly, substantially, as a person, and he is present in his entirety, as Son of God and a human being.

Eschatological Dimension of Eucharist

31 Catholics and Lutherans agree that eucharistic communion, as sacramental participation in the glorified body and blood of Christ, is a pledge that our life in Christ will be eternal, our bodies will rise, and the present world is destined for transformation, in the hope of uniting us in communion with the saints of all ages now with Christ in heaven.

Eucharist and Church

32 Lutherans and Catholics agree that sharing in the celebration of the eucharist is an essential sign of the unity of the church, and that the reality of the church as a community is realized and furthered sacramentally in the eucharistic celebration. The eucharist both mirrors and builds the church in its unity.

III. Agreements in the Lutheran–Roman Catholic Dialogues—Elaborated and Documented

A. Church

The following section sets forth findings of the Lutheran–Roman Catholic dialogues that explain and justify the agreements stated concisely in the previous section, beginning with the 12 agreements on the church.

The possibility of such a presentation on the church was foreseen as early as 1980. When the second phase of the world-level dialogue set forth the ecumenical potentialities of the Augsburg Confession on its 450th anniversary, the agreed statement formulated the following shared Lutheran–Roman Catholic notion of the church:

> A basic if still incomplete accord is also registered today even in our understanding of the church, where there were serious controversies between us in the past. By church we mean the communion of those whom God gathers together through Christ in the Holy Spirit, by the

proclamation of the gospel and the administration of the sacraments, and the ministry instituted by him for this purpose. Though it always includes sinners, yet in virtue of the promise and fidelity of God it is the one, holy, catholic and apostolic church which continues forever (CA VII and VIII). (*All Under One Christ*, §16)

From this promising starting point, the present report will now elaborate the particular ecclesiological agreements of this common view. To each of the agreements, already stated previously, the following text adds selected elucidations drawn from the dialogue documents, especially those of 1993 to 2006, in order to add theological density to the positive contents of this "basic if still incomplete accord" on the church, which, however, proves to be far more extensive than was generally thought at the time of the 1980 formulation.

1 Catholics and Lutherans agree that the church on earth has been assembled by the triune God, who grants to its members their sharing in the triune divine life as God's own people, as the body of the risen Christ, and as the temple of the Holy Spirit, while they are also called to give witness to these gifts so that others may come to share in them.

The international document, *Church and Justification* (1993), asserts that the church is a divinely created human reality, anchored in the divine life of the triune God. This precludes regarding it merely or even primarily as a human societal reality, for God assembles the church so it may share in the triune divine life (*Church and Justification*, §49).

The U.S. dialogue on *The Church as Koinonia of Salvation: Its Structures and Ministries* (2005) affirms a common "*koinonia* ecclesiology," that is, of the church both sharing in salvation, in fellowship with the Father, Son, and Holy Spirit, and called to share salvation by evangelization and a transforming mission to the world (*Church as Koinonia of Salvation*, §§11–12). The Swedish and Finnish Catholic–Lutheran dialogue of 2010 likewise asserts the church's communion with the triune God (*Justification in the Life of the Church*, §§107–12). Together, both Lutherans and Catholics consider the church according to the "master images" by which Scripture relates the church to the triune God, that is, as "pilgrim people," "body of Christ," and "temple of the Holy Spirit" (*Church and Justification*, §§48–62).[4]

Lutherans and Catholics acknowledge in faith that the church belongs to a new age of salvation history as God's pilgrim people drawn from all nations. This is a priestly people that calls upon God in prayer, serves him with all their lives, and witnesses to all people everywhere. On its journey, the people struggle against powers opposed to God, doing battle with weapons of the Spirit (Ephesians 6:10–16), while confidently following Christ who leads them toward the rest and peace of God's final kingdom (Hebrews 6:20, 12:2; *Church and Justification*, §§51–55).

The church by baptism rests on the sacramental reality of its members' real participation in Christ as the crucified and risen Lord, and so it is the body of Christ (1 Corinthians 12:12–13:27). In eucharistic communion, "we who are many are one body, for we all partake of the one bread" (1 Corinthians 10:17), which is Christ's body given for us. From Christ the

---

4. The German study *Communio Sanctorum: The Church as the Communion of Saints* develops the grounding of the communion of saints in the love of the triune God and sees it manifest in the three basic images in its ch. 3, §§23–34. The Faith and Order convergence text, *The Church: Towards a Common Vision* (2013), presents in ch. II, "The Church of the Triune God," especially in §13 ("As a divinely established communion, the Church belongs to God and does not exist for itself"), §16 (the Spirit's bestowal of faith and charisms, with the Church's essential gifts, qualities, and order), and §21 (the Church as body of Christ and temple of the Holy Spirit).

head flow the mutual services of the church's common life for building up the church and its unity (Ephesians 4:10)—by its members living together in love (1 Corinthians 13:13–14:1). Christ's members look forward to being raised by God to eternal life in communion with the risen Lord (*Church and Justification*, §§56–58).

The church is as well the temple of the Holy Spirit, the Sanctifier. The international document *The Apostolicity of the Church* states that Catholics and Lutherans are one in confessing that the church is an essential work of the Holy Spirit, who created the church through the gospel of Jesus Christ (*Apostolicity*, §147). The Holy Spirit awakens faith in those hearing the gospel and thus brings the church to exist and be endowed with manifold gifts. Beyond this, the community of believers owes its communion to the indwelling Spirit (1 Corinthians 12:13) and is to grow "into a holy temple in the Lord" (Ephesians 2:21). The one Spirit maintains the church in truth (John 14:26), but it will be complete only at the end in the New Jerusalem of which the temple is God Almighty and the Lamb (Revelation 21:22; *Church and Justification*, §§59–62).[5]

2 Catholics and Lutherans agree as well that the church on earth arose from the whole event of Jesus Christ, who remains its sole foundation (1 Corinthians 3:11).

Church and Justification (1993) affirms the shared Lutheran and Catholic conviction that the church owes its origin not to a single isolated action of institution by Christ but to the totality of the Christ-event, which extends from God sending his Son as redeemer (Galatians 4:4) through his birth and manifestation, his proclaiming of the reign of God in word and merciful

---

5. *Communio Sanctorum* gives in §28 and §§201–12 the eschatological dimensions of the church.

deed, his teaching and sharing at table with sinners, his calling and formation of disciples, his institution of the meal that memorializes his atoning death, and especially by his death on the cross and resurrection on the third day, and finally his commissioning of apostles who were empowered by the outpouring of the Holy Spirit of Pentecost to go to all nations to proclaim the gospel of Christ and his saving work (*Church and Justification*, §§10–12 and §§18–33).[6]

The 1984 document from the German dialogue, *Ecclesial Communion (Kirchengemeinschaft) in Word and Sacrament*, asserts that Lutherans and Catholics share the conviction that the church is the communion *founded by Jesus Christ*, a communion of *life with Christ* in his body as believers who are drawn into his death and rising by baptism and the Lord's supper, and a communion *in Christ* living under his presence and influence through the Holy Spirit by whom he acts as the one teacher, one high priest, and one shepherd (*Kirchengemeinschaft*, §§2–4).

3 Catholics and Lutherans hold in common that the church on earth is gathered by the proclamation of the gospel of God's saving mercy in Christ, so that the gospel, proclaimed in the Holy Spirit by the apostles, remains the church's normative origin and abiding foundation.

Church and Justification observes that the New Testament books of Acts and the proto-Pauline letters give ample witness to how Christ's apostles proclaimed the gospel of Christ by announcing his saving death and resurrection. When people heard this and accepted it in faith as a message of merciful salvation for themselves, congregations were constituted from Jerusalem as far as Rome and beyond. The primacy of the gospel is a well-known emphasis of the

---

6. Also see *DV* 4.

Reformation, expressed by calling the church "a creature of the Gospel" (*creatura Evangelii*) (*Church and Justification*, §§34-37).[7] Vatican II manifests as well the conviction that "the gospel . . . is for all time the source of life for the Church" and its preaching is "the chief means" of founding the church (*LG* 20; *AG* 6).

In every age the Holy Spirit calls and empowers witnesses to proclaim the gospel, while awakening and sustaining faith in those who hear, leading to their confessing Christ as Lord and moving confidently through him to the Father. Thus, proclaiming the gospel is a fundamental reality permanently defining the church (*Church and Justification*, §§41–43).

Apostolicity of the Church asserts that Lutherans and Catholics share, as a foundational conviction of faith, the belief that the apostolic witness is "both a normative origin and an abiding foundation" (*Apostolicity*, §148). Our dialogues repeatedly expressed and confirmed that the apostolic witness to the gospel is the normative origin of the church, which stands for all time on the foundation of the apostles. The church, amid all historical changes, is ever again referred to its apostolic origin.

4 Lutherans and Catholics agree that the church is in every age apostolic, because it is founded upon the apostles' witness to the gospel, and it continuously professes the apostolic and evangelical faith while living by mandated practices handed on from the apostles. Thus, we recognize in both our ecclesial communities the attribute of apostolicity grounded in their ongoing continuity in apostolic faith, teaching, and practices.

---

7. See WA 2, 430 and 7, 721.

The New Testament gives testimony that Jesus sent his apostles as authorized witnesses of his resurrection to make disciples in the whole world and to baptize for the forgiveness of sins (Matthew 28:1–20). The apostles assembled communities of believers holding to the gospel of Jesus Christ. The New Testament apostolic writings addressed to these communities give further instruction in faith and on ecclesial practices, while inculcating a manner of life worthy of the gospel. The ancient creeds and councils explicated the apostolic faith. Guided by the Holy Spirit, the church has constantly endeavored to remain faithful to the apostolic witness of the gospel, its normative origin and abiding foundation, along with the practices handed on from the apostles.

The Apostolicity of the Church, part 2, treats the practices coming from the apostles as contributing both to a deeper understanding of apostolicity and to a mutual recognition at a basic level of our churches as apostolic. Luther gave an expansive teaching on the endowments and marks of the church, i.e., the gospel message, baptism, the Lord's supper, the keys, calling to ministry, and public worship and confession (*Apostolicity*, §§94–95).[8] Vatican II treated tradition as a many-sided apostolic patrimony of "doctrine, life and worship," which "comprises everything that serves to make the People of God live their lives in holiness and increase their faith" (*Apostolicity*, §§114–16; *DV* 8).[9] Both elaborations concern the *shared* "elements of sanctification and truth" recognized by Vatican II's Dogmatic Constitution on the Church (*LG* 8), and then set forth in more detail as common endowments operative in the churches in §15 of the same solemn document. On the

---

8. This is based on Luther, *On Councils and the Church* (1539), WA 50, 628–44, *LW* 41, 148–67, and *Against Hanswurst* (1541), WA 51, 479–87, *LW* 41, 194–99.

9. Also see *Apostolicity*, §158.

practices, see also Agreement 6, below. Regarding apostolic preaching, "In this way the church, in her doctrine, life and worship, perpetuates and transmits to every generation all that she herself is, all that she believes" (*DV* 8).

Our continuity with the apostles' witness by our believing the gospel and professing the apostolic faith is not a human achievement but a gift of the Holy Spirit, who makes and maintains the whole ecclesial body as apostolic, through the apostolic Scriptures, the faithful teachers, the creeds, and the continuity of appointed ministers (*Church as Koinonia of Salvation*, §§75–77). The church of every age is "the work of the Holy Spirit who makes present the apostolic gospel and makes effective the sacraments and apostolic instruction which we have been graced to receive" (*Apostolicity*, §147). The church in our day is called to serve the further transmission of the apostolic gospel.

Drawing on the writings of Luther on the means of grace and marks of the church and on Vatican II regarding tradition, the church, and ecumenism, Lutherans and Catholics today "mutually recognize, at a fundamental level, the presence of apostolicity in our traditions" (*Apostolicity*, §§157–60, quoting §160). Luther contributed to this insight when "he insisted that a manifold Christian substance must be recognized in the Roman Catholic Church" (*Apostolicity*, §159), for he perceived there "the true Holy Scriptures, true baptism, the true sacrament [of the altar], the true keys for forgiveness of sins, the true office of proclamation, and the true catechism."[10] Vatican II's Decree on Ecumenism asserted that "the elements of sanctification and truth" are found in the separated communities, and "the Spirit

---

10. Luther, *Concerning Rebaptism* (1528), WA 26, 146f., *LW* 40, 231f., cited in *Apostolicity of the Church*, §99.

of Christ has not refrained from using them as a means of salvation" (*UR* 3). Consequently, there is a mutual recognition: "The Catholic Church and the churches and ecclesial communities of the Reformation both participate in the attribute of apostolicity because they are built up and live by many of the same 'elements and endowments' pertaining to the one and multiple apostolic tradition" (*Apostolicity*, §121).[11]

5 Catholics and Lutherans agree that the church on earth lives from and is ruled by the Word of God, which it encounters in Christ, in the living word of the gospel, and in the inspired and canonical Scriptures.

Lutherans and Catholics agree that in human history, through words and deeds, God issued a message of grace and truth, which culminated in the saving death and resurrection of Jesus Christ. Empowered by the Holy Spirit, Easter witnesses testified to the resurrection of Jesus Christ, who is God's definitive word of grace (*Apostolicity*, §432). This Easter witness stands in continuity with God's revelation through Moses, the prophets and the Old Testament writings.[12] God's revelation of human salvation in Jesus Christ continues to be announced in the gospel of Christ that the apostles first preached and taught when they gathered communities of believers.

---

11. Part 2 of *Apostolicity* notes at the end that the mutual recognition it has set forth is presently "limited on both sides by significant reservations about the doctrine and church life of the partner in dialogue" (§161). The reservations concern differences, first, over "ordination to the pastorate, ministry in apostolic succession, and the office of bishop in the church." A second area of reservations concerns the authentic interpretation of Scripture and the structure and function of the teaching office (§162). However, Parts 3 and 4 of *Apostolicity* give these two topics ample treatment, which show real progress toward, but not the achievement of, reconciliation of the differences.

12. *Nostra Aetate*, Declaration on the Relationship of the Church to Non-Christian Religions 4, quoted in *Church and Justification* 2.2, §13.

The world-level ecumenical document *Apostolicity of the Church* (2006) asserts:

> The Scriptures are for Lutherans and Catholics the source, rule, guideline, and criterion of correctness and purity of the church's proclamation, of its elaboration of doctrine, and of its sacramental and pastoral practice. For in the midst of the first communities formed by Christ's apostles, the New Testament books emerged, under the Holy Spirit's inspiration, through the preaching and teaching of the apostolic gospel. These books, together with the sacred books of Israel in the Old Testament, are to make present for all ages the truth of God's word, so as to form faith and guide believers in a life worthy of the gospel of Christ. By the biblical canon, the church does not constitute, but instead recognizes, the inherent authority of the prophetic and apostolic Scriptures. Consequently, the church's preaching and whole life must be nourished and ruled by the Scriptures constantly heard and studied. True interpretation and application of Scripture maintains church teaching in the truth. (*Apostolicity*, §434)

The church of every age stands under the imperative to preserve in continuous succession God's words of saving truth. Made bold by Christ's promise to be with his disciples always, the church carries out Christ's mandate to announce his gospel in every place from generation to generation (*Apostolicity*, §433).

6 Catholics and Lutherans are one in holding that the church on earth participates in Christ's benefits through the historical and perceptible actions of proclaiming the gospel and

celebrating the sacraments, as initiated by Christ and handed on by his apostles.

World-level (*Apostolicity of the Church*) and national dialogues (*Kirchengemeinschaft in Wort und Sakrament* and *Communio Sanctorum*) have asserted that Lutherans and Catholics have profound agreement on the essential role of the means of grace in assembling the church and communicating to its members ever anew a share in God's saving gifts.

The proclaimed gospel has a primacy among the mediations of communion in Christ and his benefits, but receiving it in faith entails as well receiving the sacramental practices of baptism, the Lord's supper or eucharist, and absolution from sin—all as administered by those called to the ministry of word and sacrament. By these "means of grace," the message of Christ engages with divine power the whole of human life with the forgiveness of sins, deepened union with Christ, and sanctification through the Holy Spirit. These means are also significant external, public "marks" of the community living in continuity with what Christ and his apostles instituted.[13]

7 Catholics and Lutherans agree that the church on earth is a communion (*koinonia*). It shares in God's gifts offered for us by Christ, which, by being held in common, bring believers into unity and fellowship with each other.

---

13. *Kirchengemeinschaft in Wort und Sakrament*, §7; *Communio Sanctorum*, §§35–38, which introduce the ample treatment in ch. 4 of "The Communion of Saints through Word and Sacrament"; *Apostolicity*, §§94–95 and §§157–60, states the agreement on the practices embodying the saving gospel message. Also see *LG* 8 "on the many elements of sanctification of truth" which are shared by Christians not withstanding our divisions. These elements are described in greater detail in LG 15: sacred Scripture as a rule of faith and life; "the belief in God the Father Almighty and in Christ, the Son of God and the Savior"; baptism; prayer; and spiritual benefits uniting us by the Holy Spirit's sanctifying power.

In the past, the conceptions of the church held by Lutherans and Catholics developed along diverging paths, but in the 20th century we have together appropriated the biblical notion of *koinonia* and applied it to the church in a process giving us a precious communality.[14] *Church and Justification* (§§63–73) describes the church on earth as sharing in a *koinonia* or communion founded in the Trinity. *The Church as Koinonia of Salvation: Its Structures and Ministries* has shown the wide-ranging fruitfulness of communion ecclesiology for the dialogue on the church and its ministries.

The communion formed from the agreement and common intentions of believers with each other does not constitute the church; rather, the church is formed by the message of Christ proclaimed in the power of the Holy Spirit. When the Spirit awakens faith in the gospel as the good news of redemption, this message is confessed in common by people who thereby come together as sharers in it and its saving power (*Church and Justification*, §65 and §67).[15]

Baptism shows the priority of God's action in calling people to be his own as they are consecrated in the name of Father, Son, and Holy Spirit and incorporated into the already existing body of Christ (*Church and Justification*, §68). At Holy Communion, believers receive from the "cup of blessing" which is their sharing (*koinonia*) in the blood of Christ. The "breaking of the bread" leads to sharing (*koinonia*) in the body of Christ, which makes

---

14. *Communio Sanctorum*, §§23–24, indicates the breadth of *communion* thinking in several churches and ecumenical dialogues. *The Church as Koinonia of Salvation* introduces basic themes of *koinonia* in §§10–14 and relates the steps of its recent adoption by Catholics and Lutherans in §§15–20.

15. *The Church: Towards a Common Vision* states in §23 that the church is not merely the sum of individual believers among themselves but "fundamentally a communion in the Triune God and, at the same time, a communion whose members partake together in the mission of God (cf. 2 Pet. 1:4), who as Trinity, is the source and focus of all communion."

the many one body in Christ (1 Corinthians 10:16–17; *Church and Justification*, §§69–70).

8 Catholics and Lutherans agree that the church on earth combines audible and visible elements with profound spiritual realities that remain hidden from empirical investigation and perception.

Previous agreements of this *Declaration* have concerned essential audible realities of the church, such as the proclaimed gospel by which the church is gathered (no. 3) and the church's continuous profession of the apostolic and evangelical faith (no. 4). The latter agreement, echoing also later (in no. 6), affirms as well the central role in both of our churches of practices with perceptible, embodied components, such as baptism, the Lord's supper or eucharist, exercising the keys for the forgiveness of sins, and designating and ordaining members for the pastoral office of preaching, sacramental celebration, and pastoral care. A further perceptible element at the very center of the lives of believers and communities in both our churches are the Scriptures that we take to be inspired and canonical (no. 5).

Also both our traditions avoid identifying the church exclusively with visible structures and outward manifestations. Although some early Lutheran polemics rejected identifying the church with the ordained hierarchy, Lutherans have always denied that the church is a kind of "Platonic republic." Instead, the church can be seen where an assembly has the visible "marks" of the word, confession, and sacraments (*Church and Justification*, §§69–70).[16]

---

16. See WA 40/II, 106, 19; *LW* 27, 84. Apology of the Augsburg Confession, 7, 20 (no "Platonic republic") and 7, 3 (the marks). See also *Apostolicity*, §§94–95.

Post-Reformation Catholics were concerned to avoid priori-
tizing an exclusively spiritual reality of the church and consequently emphasized the church as a visible reality marked
by creed, sacramental structure, and hierarchical leadership.
But Catholics also affirm an indissoluble link between the visible assembly and the mystery of its life shared in communion
with God, which is the spiritual and transcendent reality of the
church. This and the visible social community relate to each
other in a manner analogous to the relation between Christ's
divine and human natures, which are inseparable but distinct.
In the church, the ecclesial society never fully envelops the
"community of salvation" (*Church and Justification*, §144; LG 8
and *UR* 3).

Lutherans and Catholics agree that in this world the profound
reality of the church, which is sharing the triune divine life in
Christ and with Christ (Nos. 1 and 2, above), is hidden. Only
the eye of faith can recognize that an assembly is indeed an
assembly of the people of God where God is at work through
word and sacrament. The salvation community of believers
in Christ, made one body in Christ and a temple of the Holy
Spirit (No. 1, above), is not recognizable by earthly standards,
and furthermore it remains hidden because sin, which is also
present in the church, makes ascertaining the community of
salvation's membership uncertain (*Church and Justification*,
§§140–41, and 147).[17]

9 Catholics and Lutherans agree that the church on earth is
indefectible, because it is and will be preserved by the Holy
Spirit in all aspects essential for salvation. We share the certainty of Christian hope that the church, established by Christ

---

17. In agreements to follow, further hidden realities will be matters of agreement,
e.g., no. 8 on "divine gifts and conditions of blessings, righteousness, and truth,"
and no. 10 on "the church's communion with the saints in glory."

and led by his Spirit, will always remain in the truth, fulfilling its mission to humanity for the sake of the gospel.

Catholics and Lutherans have taken to heart the risen Christ's promise "to be with you always, until the end of the age" (Matthew 28:20). Accordingly, we believe firmly that with the continued assistance of the risen Christ through the Holy Spirit the church will remain until the end of time (CA VII; *LG* 20). Its indefectibility includes its perseverance in the truth of the gospel, in its life of faith, and in its mission.

The Common Statement of U.S. dialogue, Round VI, *Teaching Authority and Infallibility in the Church* (1978), asserts: "Lutheran and Catholic traditions share the certainty of Christian hope that the Church, established by Christ and led by his Spirit, will always remain in the truth fulfilling its mission to humanity for the sake of the Gospel" (§28). The document identified places of significant convergences related to God's preservation of the church in the truth:

> The context within which the Catholic doctrine of papal infallibility is understood has changed. Lutherans and Catholics now speak in increasingly similar ways about the gospel and its communication, about the authority of Christian truth, and about how to settle disputes concerning the understanding of the Christian message. One can truly speak of a convergence between our two traditions. The following instances of this convergence are significant. Our churches are agreed . . . that in accordance with the promises given in the Scriptures and because of the continued assistance of the risen Christ through the Holy Spirit, the Church will remain until the end of time; that this perpetuity of the Church includes its indefectibility, i.e., its perseverance in the truth of the gospel, in its mission, and in its life of faith; that among the means by

which Christ preserves the Church in the truth of the gospel, there is the Ministry of the Word and sacrament, which will never perish from the Church. (§41)

Among the means by which Christ, the Lord of the church, preserves his church in the truth of the gospel, Lutherans and Catholics attribute great importance to the ministry of word and sacrament, which is charged with faithful transmission of the gospel and teaching of Christian doctrine. This service will never perish from the church.

Indefectible fidelity to the truth necessary for salvation is not an automatic, all-embracing quality of everything that church leaders say or endorse but is the result of the Holy Spirit's guidance (cf. John 16:13), which is recognized by testing the church's faith and life by the standard of the word of God.

10 Catholics and Lutherans agree that the church on earth is united with the community of the saints in glory.

Church and Justification asserts:

> The *communio* with God which has already been given and realized on earth through Jesus Christ in the Holy Spirit is the foundation of Christian hope beyond death and of the *communio* between Christ's saints on earth and Christ's saints who have already died. . . . We believe in the fundamental indestructibility of the life given us in Christ through the power of the Holy Spirit even through the judgment and beyond death. (§295)

A similar conviction is found in the document from the German bilateral dialogue, *Communio Sanctorum: The Church as the Communion of Saints* (2000): "The communion in Christ into which human beings are called endures also in death and judgment. It becomes complete as, through the pain over failure in earthly life, persons come with their love to give the perfect response to God" (§228).

The U.S. Dialogue Round XI document, *The Hope of Eternal Life* (2010), asserts:

> "The fellowship of those sanctified, the 'holy ones' or saints, includes believers both living and dead. There is thus a solidarity of the church throughout the world with the church triumphant." This solidarity across the barrier of death is particularly evident in the Eucharist, which is always celebrated in unity with the hosts of heaven. . . . Particularly in praise and adoration of God at the Lord's table, the apparent division marked by death melts away. (§217)[18]

Pope John Paul II's statement *Ut unum sint* (1995) applies to this relationship, for "the communion between our Communities, even if still incomplete, is truly and solidly grounded in the full communion of the Saints—those who, at the end of a life faithful to grace, are in communion with Christ in glory. These Saints come from all the Churches and Ecclesial Communities which gave them entrance into the communion of salvation."[19]

11 Catholics and Lutherans agree that the church on earth is an anticipatory reality, on pilgrimage and expectant of reaching its final destination in God's ultimate gathering of his

---

18. The first two sentences cite the U.S. dialogue, Round VII, *The One Mediator, the Saints, and Mary* (1990), §103. *Church and Justification* (1993) had stated in §296, "The communion of saints, the unity of the pilgrim and heavenly church, is realized especially in worship, in the adoration and praise of the thrice-holy God and the Lamb, our Lord Jesus Christ (cf. Revelation 4:2–11; 5:9–14)."

19. John Paul II, *Ut unum sint*, Encyclical Letter on Commitment to Ecumenism, May 25, 1995 (Ascension Thursday), §84.

people in their entirety when Christ returns and when the Holy Spirit completes the work of sanctification.

The "master images" by which the church is designated in relation to the three persons of the Trinity (pilgrim people of God, body of Christ, temple of the Holy Spirit) each point to a future consummation of what the church is now in an anticipatory fashion or proleptically. The people of God look forward to completing their pilgrimage in a great gathering of all the redeemed on the final day. The members of Christ's body believe he will return in glory to be manifested as head of the final communion of saints. The Holy Spirit's present sanctification is authentic, while also being "the first fruits" or "down payment" (*arrabōn*: Romans 8:23; 2 Corinthians 1:22; 5:5; Ephesians 1:14) of holiness in eschatological completion (*Church and Justification*, §§72–73).[20]

While the church is already partaking (*koinonia*) in the saving gifts and conditions deriving from the common life and merciful approach of Father, Son, and Holy Spirit, it has these in fragmentary and incomplete ways. They now instill hope and joy but also anticipation and longing for them in the manner of their consummation in the final kingdom of God, when the triune God will be "all in all" (1 Corinthians 15:24–28).[21]

12 Catholics and Lutherans agree that the church on earth is mandated to carry out a mission in which it participates in God's activity in the world by evangelization, worship, service of humanity, and care for creation.

The church's ultimate goal is consummation in God's kingdom, for God will create an eternal reign of righteousness,

---

20. Also see *Communio Sanctorum*, §203, and the section "Our Common Hope," in Round XI of the U.S. dialogue, *The Hope of Eternal Life* (2010), §§15–19.

21. Cf. 1 Corinthians 1:7–9; *LG* §§7, 48–51.

peace, and love. Through grace, God has chosen and established the church *in* this age and *for* this age to proclaim the gospel to all people, worship God, and make Christ known through care and service to others (*Church and Justification*, §243). *Church and Justification* (1993) identifies major and extensive areas of agreement on the church's mission:

> Catholics and Lutherans are agreed that the mission of the church to proclaim the gospel and serve humanity is a true—even if limited—sharing in God's activity in the world toward the realization of his plan as Creator, Redeemer, and Sanctifier. (§256)

> Lutherans and Catholics are agreed on the priority of the task of evangelizing the world, on the central significance of proclaiming and celebrating the grace of God in worship, and on the commandment to serve humanity as a whole. They also agree that "*martyria, leitourgia,* and *diakonia* (witness, worship and service to the neighbor) are tasks entrusted to the whole people of God." (§277)[22]

The German dialogue study *Communio Sanctorum* (2000) presented the church as sign and instrument of salvation, to which it added common clarifying statements that "the church is in its entire existence a sign of the saving will of God, who desires 'that all people be saved and come to see the truth' (1 Timothy 2:4)," and that "the church remains constantly subject to the Lord, and salvation remains a gift of God, even in the work of the church" (§89).

Church and Justification spoke of the missionary imperative, asserting that the gospel message of grace and reconciliation

---

22. This quotation incorporates a passage from the earlier world-level dialogue, *The Ministry in the Church* (1982), §13.

compels those who have heard and accepted it to bring it to those who have not heard it or who have still no proper opportunity to accept it: "We must be alarmed when we think about those who have forgotten or estranged themselves from God's good news. Catholics and Lutherans together must accept their missionary calling as disciples of Jesus Christ. They must in common face the challenges of constant renewal in their churches under the influence of the Holy Spirit, so that they become common instruments for God's saving plan in more authentic ways" (*Church and Justification*, §248).

Communio Sanctorum, completed in 2000 shortly after the signing of the *Joint Declaration on the Doctrine of Justification*, indicated the contemporary urgency of the mission of a common Lutheran–Catholic witness to the message of justification:

> The more confusing the variety of religious and pseudo-religious options in our world becomes, the more important it is that our churches publicly bear witness together to the love of God for all people. The more an atmosphere of vanishing trust toward one another spreads throughout our society, the more helpful it will be for many uncertain people seeking support and help if Christians are able to speak with one voice, with personal certainty of faith, about the unchanging and limitless faithfulness of God with regard to his promises of salvation. (*Communio sanctorum*, §119)

Church and Justification asserted the centrality of worship, for the church on earth is called to join in praise and intercession. In worship we are linked with Christians of every age. In the midst of our worship, faith is induced and nourished through sacramental life and the proclamation of the gospel:

When we gather together to confess our sins, to hear God's saving word, to remember his great deeds, and to sing hymns and songs, to intercede for a blessing on everyone and to celebrate the eucharistic meal, we are a people of faith in the most pregnant sense. This is our proper task as church, and we accept it as such with a sense of responsibility to offer our Creator and Redeemer adoration and praise in the name of all creatures. (*Church and Justification*, §284)

The church on earth is likewise called to serve humanity and all creation: "As Christians and as communities we are instruments of God in the service of mercy and justice in the world" (*Church and Justification*, §285). In obedience to Christ, who took the form of a servant (Philippians 2:7), we are called to service by contributing to the world's preservation and well-being:

By striving in common with all people of good will for healing, protection and promotion of human dignity, for respectful and rational handling of the resources of creation, for the consolidation of social unity, respect for social diversity and for deepening of the general sense of responsibility, Christians are servants of the Creator's love for the world. (*Church and Justification*, §286)

Christian service to humanity and the world includes championing human dignity and inviolable human rights, providing generous aid in situations of special distress, and working on projects directed toward promoting long-term solutions to overcome misery (*Church and Justification*, §§287–88). Christians—in their various callings and spheres of activity—are called to make contributions "in all areas of social life—in politics, education and nurture, health, science, culture and the mass media" to "promote lives in accord with human dignity and reverence toward God" (*Church and Justification*, §289).[23]

B. Ministry

Lutherans and Catholics find that questions concerning ministry pose especially formidable obstacles in the way toward growth in communion, as they have frequently in ecumenical relationships.[24] Ecclesiological and eucharistic differences often become evident in relationship to ministry. Without movement on these questions, therefore, agreements in other areas cannot fully bear their fruit in shared worship and witness.

Yet it is important to recognize how theological dialogues between Catholics and Lutherans have allowed agreements to be claimed for many questions concerning ministry. What once seemed to be long-standing, sharply defined contrasting positions have yielded to insights from shared historical inquiry, theological reexaminations within each tradition, and more accurate knowledge of one another's practices. This ecumenical progress has allowed measured and nuanced understandings to emerge on crucial topics surrounding the mutual recognition of ministry. This trajectory from opposition to growing convergence appeared early in recommendations

---

23. This account in several places echoes *The Church: Towards a Common Vision*, especially §24, on the church serving God's goal of gathering humanity and all of creation under Christ's lordship, while manifesting God's mercy to human beings, §§58–59, on the church intended by God not for its own sake but to serve the divine plan for the transformation of the world by evangelizing and promoting justice and peace, and §§64–66, on the church's actions in society.

24. For example, *The Church: Towards a Common Vision*, the 2013 paper on ecclesiology from the Faith and Order Commission of the World Council of Churches, notes, "Ecumenical dialogue has repeatedly shown that issues relating to ordained ministry constitute challenging obstacles on the path to unity. If [such] differences . . . prohibit full unity, it must continue to be an urgent priority for the churches to discover how they can be overcome" (p. 26).

regarding ministry. Thus, the second phase of international dialogue (1981) focused on questions of ministry identified by the *Malta Report* in 1972, while the U.S. dialogue had moved from *The Eucharist as Sacrifice* (1967) to a substantial and forward-looking examination of *Eucharist and Ministry* in 1979. More recently, the U.S. statement *The Church as Koinonia of Salvation* and the international study document *Apostolicity of the Church* addressed many questions regarding ministry. Together, these dialogue reports identify a number of ways in which Lutherans and Catholics can take specific steps toward a mutual recognition of ministry.

Agreement between Lutherans and Catholics on the doctrine of justification helped give new impetus for further attention to the dividing issues of ministry. Already the *Malta Report* had indicated how the topics could be linked:

> The question of the office of the ministry in the church, its origin, its position and correct understanding represents one of the most important open questions between Lutherans and Catholics. It is here that the question of the position of the gospel in and over the church becomes concrete. What, in other words, are the consequences of the doctrine of justification for the understanding of the ministerial office? (§47)

The 2010 Finnish–Swedish regional report, *Justification in the Life of the Church*, was shaped throughout by the dialogue's guiding question, "What is the place of justification in the life of our respective churches?" Thus, the church's ministry was considered as it is "in the service of justification." To see it in this way was a response to the final paragraph of the *Joint Declaration*:

> Our consensus in basic truths of the doctrine of justification must come to influence the life and teachings of our

churches. Here it must prove itself. In this respect, there are still questions of varying importance which need further clarification . . . [including] ministry. . . . We are convinced that the consensus we have reached offers a solid basis for this clarification. The Lutheran churches and the Roman Catholic Church will continue to strive together to deepen this common understanding of justification and to make it bear fruit in the life and teaching of the churches. (§43)

The connection between the *Joint Declaration on the Doctrine of Justification* and the topic of ministry includes first, the applicability of the ecumenical method of differentiating consensus to ministry, and, second, the intrinsic relationship between the doctrine of justification and ministry. Regarding ecumenical method, the international dialogue report *The Apostolicity of the Church* already had indicated several ways forward. It directly appealed to how the ecumenical method of differentiating consensus might be extended to questions of ministry. While also recognizing the distinctiveness of this topic, because it involves ecclesial practice as well as doctrine, the dialogue commission said, "One has to ask whether a differentiated consensus is not possible as well in the doctrine of the ministry or ministries." Indeed, the dialogue invites Lutherans and Catholics to consider whether the differentiating consensus achieved for the doctrine of justification could be paralleled by "an approach to the differing forms of ministry, in which one discovers so much common ground that reciprocal recognition of ministries would be possible" (§292).

With respect to the intrinsic relationship between the doctrine of justification and ministry, the report explained:

> For apostolic succession, succession in faith is the essential aspect. . . . But now, the *Joint Declaration on the Doctrine*

of Justification has ascertained . . . between the Catholic Church and Lutheran churches . . . a high degree of agreement in faith, that is, in that which represents the heart of apostolic succession. . . . **The Catholic view of the ministry of the Lutheran churches, along with the Lutheran view of ministry in the Roman Catholic Church, cannot remain untouched by the** *Joint Declaration*. For, even if preserving correct doctrine is not the task of the ordained ministry alone, it is still its specific task to teach and proclaim the gospel publicly. The signing of the *Joint Declaration* therefore implies the acknowledgment that the ordained ministry in both churches has by the power of the Holy Spirit fulfilled its service of maintaining fidelity to the apostolic gospel regarding the central question of faith set forth in the Declaration. (*Apostolicity* 288; emphasis added)

13 Lutherans and Catholics agree that the ordained ministry belongs to the essential elements that express the church's apostolic character and that it also contributes, through the power of the Holy Spirit, to the church's continuing apostolic faithfulness (cf. *Apostolicity*, §271).

The comprehensive examination of apostolicity presented by the fourth phase of world-level dialogue examined "the 'elements' which, by the power of the Holy Spirit, contribute to building up the church 'upon the foundation of the apostles and prophets, with Christ Jesus himself as the cornerstone' (Ephesians 2:20). Among these elements are the Holy Scriptures, the communication of God's word in proclamation, baptism, and the Lord's Supper, the office of the keys, catechesis as transmission of the apostolic tradition, the Creeds, the Lord's Prayer, and the Ten Commandments." These elements, which are truly "institutions and enactments of the communication of the word of God in which the content of the apostolic gospel becomes present to bring salvation to human beings," can play their parts in maintaining the apostolicity of the church only by involving human beings. Thus, *Apostolicity* asserts, "There is no testimony without a witness, no sermon without a preacher, no administration of the sacraments without a minister, but also no testimony and no sermon without people who listen, no celebration of the sacraments without people who receive them" (§165).

14 Catholics and Lutherans agree that all the baptized who believe in Christ share in the priesthood of Christ. For both Catholics and Lutherans, the common priesthood of all the baptized and the special, ordained ministry enhance one another.

The Ministry in the Church affirmed that "*martyria, leiturgia* and *diakonia* (witness, worship and service to the neighbor) are tasks entrusted to the whole people of God. . . . Through baptism all constitute the one priestly people of God (1 Peter 2:5, 9; Revelation 1:6; 5:10). While consciousness of the calling of the whole people of God had sometimes been neglected "in both our churches," recent discussions have restored its prominence for ecclesiology and for the theology of ministry. Thus, it is possible to affirm that "the doctrine of the common priesthood of all the baptized and of the serving character of the ministries in the church and for the church represents in our day a joint starting point for Lutherans and Catholics" (§15).

For both Catholics and Lutherans, there can be no competition between these two dimensions of the church's life. "Instead, the special ministry is precisely service to the common priesthood of all . . . so that the faithful can, each in his or her own place, be priests in the sense of the universal priesthood and fulfill the mission of the church in that place" (*Apostolicity*, §275). Properly understood, then, "there is a differentiated referential relationship between the specific tasks of the general priesthood of all the baptized and of the ordained ministry" (§254).

15 Lutherans and Catholics affirm together that ordained ministry is of divine origin and that it is necessary for the being of the church. Ministry is not simply a delegation "from below," but is instituted by Jesus Christ.

Referring to the "ministry of leadership" already evident from New Testament times, the 1981 international dialogue said, "In continuous relation to the normative apostolic tradition, it [the ministry] makes present the mission of Jesus Christ. The presence of this ministry in the community 'signifies the priority of divine initiative and authority in the Church's existence.' Consequently, this ministry is not simply a delegation 'from below,' but is instituted by Jesus Christ" (*Ministry*, §20; the quotation is from *Baptism, Eucharist, and Ministry*, §14).

Similarly, *The Apostolicity of the Church* declared, "Catholics and Lutherans affirm together that God instituted the ministry and that it is necessary for the being of the Church, since the word of God and its public proclamation in word and sacrament are necessary for faith in Jesus Christ to arise and be preserved and together with this for the church to come into being and be preserved as believers who make up the body of Christ in the unity of faith" (§276; also found in *From Conflict to Communion*, §178).

According to contemporary understanding, to say that ministry is "instituted by Jesus Christ" generally does not point to a single act of Jesus or to one scriptural text but rather affirms that the ministry of the church reflects God's will and carries out the mission of Christ (cf. *Apostolicity*, §281).

16 We both affirm that all ministry is subordinated to Christ, who in the Holy Spirit is acting in the preaching of the

word of God, in the administration of the sacraments, and in pastoral service.

The Ministry in the Church declares of ecclesial life, "Within this priestly people of God, Christ, acting through the Holy Spirit, confers manifold ministries: apostles, prophets, evangelists, pastors and teachers 'to equip the saints for the work of ministry, for building up the body of Christ' (Ephesians 4:11f.). Called into the ministry of reconciliation, and as those being entrusted with the word of reconciliation, they are 'ambassadors in Christ's stead' (cf. 2 Corinthians 5:18–20); yet they are not lords over the faith but ministers of joy (2 Corinthians 1:24)" (§14).

Thus, Lutherans and Catholics can both affirm that all ministry is subordinated to Christ, who "in the Holy Spirit, is acting in the preaching of the word of God, in the administration of the sacraments, and in the pastoral service. Jesus Christ, acting in the present, takes the minister into his service; the minister is only his tool and instrument. Jesus Christ is the one and only high priest of the New Covenant" (*Ministry*, §21, *Apostolicity*, §274).

17 Lutherans and Catholics agree that the proclamation of the gospel is foremost among the various tasks of the ordained ministry.

Already the *Malta Report* reported increased mutual appreciation on this subject:

> The Second Vatican Council has emphasized in a new way that the basic task of priests is the proclamation of the gospel. Further, it is stressed in the administration of the sacraments that these sacraments are of the faith which are born from the word and nourished by the word. According to the

Lutheran Confessions, it is the task of the ministerial office to proclaim the gospel and administer the sacraments in accordance with the gospel so that in this way faith is awakened and strengthened. Over against an earlier one-sided emphasis on proclamation, the sacraments in the Lutheran churches are currently coming to have a more important place in the spiritual life of the congregations. (§61; the references are to Vatican II's Decree on the Ministry and Life of Priests, *PO* §4, and to the Augsburg Confession V, VII)

Apostolicity of the Church reiterated this point: "[F]or both Catholics and Lutherans the fundamental duty and intention of the ordained ministry is public service of the Word of God, the gospel of Jesus Christ, which the Triune God has commissioned the church to proclaim to all the world. Every office and every office-holder must be measured against this obligation" (§274).

18 We declare in common that the essential and specific function of the ordained minister is to assemble and build up the Christian community by proclaiming the word of God; celebrating the sacraments; and presiding over the liturgical, missionary, and diaconal life of the community.

After surveying historical differences in "starting points" and emphasis in understanding ordained ministry, *The Ministry in the Church* was able to conclude, "Our churches are thus able today to declare *in common* that the essential and specific function of the ordained minister is to assemble and build up the Christian community by proclaiming the word of God, celebrating the sacraments, and presiding over the liturgical, missionary, and diaconal life of the community" (§31). The echo here of the language in the document from the World Council of Churches, *Baptism, Eucharist, and Ministry*, is striking: "The chief responsibility of the ordained ministry is to assemble and build up the body of Christ by proclaiming and teaching the Word of God, by celebrating the sacraments, and by guiding the life of the community in its worship, its mission and its caring ministry" (*Ministry*, §13).

19 The authority of the ministry is not to be understood as an individual possession of the minister, but it is rather an authority with the commission to serve in the community and for the community.

Referring to all ministries, the international dialogue commission said in 1981, "They render their service in the midst of the whole people and for the people of God which, as a whole, is the 'one, holy, catholic and apostolic Church'" (*Ministry*, §14). Referring to ordained ministry in particular, this dialogue specified that its authority is "not to be understood as an individual possession of the minister, but it is rather an authority with the commission to serve in the community and for the community. Therefore, the exercise of the authority of the ministry should involve the participation of the whole community. This applies also to the appointment of the ministers." The ordained minister "manifests and exercises the authority of Christ in the way Christ himself revealed God's authority to the world: in and through communion. For this reason the ministry must not suppress Christian freedom and fraternity but should rather promote them. The Christian freedom, fraternity, and responsibility of the whole church and of all its members must find its expression in the conciliar, collegial and synodical structures of the church" (*Ministry*, §23).

20 We also agree that the office of ministry stands over against (*gegenüber*) the community as well as within it and thus is called to exercise authority over the community.

The language of "over against" appears already in the *Malta Report*: "The correct determination of the relationship between this ministry assigned to the entire church and a special office in the church is a problem for Lutherans and Catholics alike. Both agree that the office of the ministry stands over against the community as well as within the community. Further they agree that the ministerial office represents Christ and his over-againstness to the community only insofar as it gives expression to the gospel. Both must examine themselves as to how effectively the critical superiority of the gospel is maintained in practice" (§50).

Citing this affirmation, *The Ministry in the Church* expanded the point: "For Lutherans and Catholics it is fundamental to a proper understanding of the ministerial office that 'the office of the ministry stands over against the community as well as within the community.' Inasmuch as the ministry is exercised on behalf of Jesus Christ and makes him present, it has authority over against the community. 'He who hears you hears me' (Luke 10:16). The authority of the ministry must therefore not be understood as delegated by the community" (§22).

21 Both Lutherans and Catholics affirm that entry into this apostolic and God-given ministry is by ordination, that ministers cannot ordain themselves or claim this office as a matter of right but are called by God and designated in and through the church.

The language of this Agreement is from the U.S. dialogue *Eucharist and Ministry*, §18. The affirmation recognizes both the divine initiative and the ecclesial setting of ordained ministry. *The Apostolicity of the Church* elaborated these points: "Christ himself acts in the human rite of ordination," which is "essentially induction into the ministry of the whole church, even though the present divisions of the churches prevent this from being fully realized through their call and commission. The ordained are claimed for lifelong service of the gospel" (§277).

22 Catholics and Lutherans both ordain through prayer invoking the Holy Spirit and the laying on of hands by another ordained person. Both affirm that the ordinand receives an anointing of the Holy Spirit, who equips that person for ordained ministry.

The Ministry in the Church described the common "understanding and practice of ordination," which provides the basis for "substantial convergence" between Lutheran and Catholic churches:

> Since apostolic times the calling to special ministry in the church has taken place through the laying on of hands and through prayer in the midst of the congregation assembled for worship. In this way the ordained person is received into the apostolic ministry of the church and into the community of ordained ministers. At the same time, through the laying on of hands and through prayer (*epiclesis*), the gift of the Holy Spirit is offered and conveyed for the exercise of ministry. (§32)

23 Both Lutherans and Catholics regard ordination as unrepeatable.

"By means of ordination Christ calls the ordained person once and for all into the ministry in his church. Both in the Catholic and in the Lutheran understanding, therefore, ordination can be received only once and cannot be repeated" (*Ministry*, §36). For this international dialogue, convergence on this central point, a "uniqueness which cannot be given up," grounded a consensus on the reality of ordination (§39).

Catholics have used language of *character indelebilis* for what is received at ordination. This language links ordination to baptism and confirmation, also sacraments which "impress a sign" that orders a person's position in the church. As *Ministry* explained, "In contemporary Catholic doctrinal statements, the *character indelebilis* is again understood more in terms of the promise and mission which permanently mark the ordained and claim them for the service of Christ" (§37). For Lutherans, who have often avoided what they saw as ontological and metaphysical claims in the language of *character indelebilis*, still "ordination to the ministry of the church on behalf of Christ, conferred in the power of the Holy Spirit, is for life and not subject to temporal limitations" (§38; see also *Eucharist and Ministry*, §17).

24 Both Lutherans and Catholics consider that there is one ministerial office, while also distinguishing a special ministry of *episkope* over presbyters/pastors.

For Catholics, the one sacrament of order has been apportioned among three ministries or major orders: deacon, priest (presbyter), and bishop. Even though this structure evolved during the apostolic age or later, Catholics understand this basic structure to be irreversible and belonging to the fullness of the nature of the church (*Apostolicity*, §281). For Catholics, priests are "sharers in a special way in Christ's priesthood and, by carrying out sacred functions, act as ministers of him who through his Spirit continually exercises his priesthood role for our benefit in the liturgy" (*PO* 5, cited in *Apostolicity*, §274).

Catholics hold that the fullness of ordained ministry is conferred through episcopal consecration (*LG* 21). The bishop exercises *episkope* at the regional level, the diocese, while most often, a priest is the pastor of a local parish. In the present life of the church, only bishops can ordain to the episcopacy, the presbyterate, and the diaconate. The apostolic succession of bishops manifests and serves the apostolic tradition of the church. The episcopal college is a successor of the college of the apostles (*LG* 19). Since Vatican II, the episcopate is "the basic form of ministry and the point of departure for the theological interpretation of church ministry" (*Apostolicity*, §241).

Nevertheless, for Catholic theology, there is one sacrament of order. As *The Church as Koinonia of Salvation* said, "Both bishops and presbyters are priests; priests are associated with their bishop in one presbyterium. What these ministries share is much greater than that which distinguishes them" (*The Church as Koinonia of Salvation*, §94).

The Lutheran tradition has one order of ordained ministers, usually called pastors, which can combine features that Catholics divide between the episcopate and the presbyterate. The pastor who has received this ministry possesses the fullness of that which ordination confers (*Eucharist and Ministry* §21). Yet Lutherans do not reject the division of the one office into different ministries which has developed in the history of the church. The Augsburg Confession affirms the desire of the Lutheran reformers to preserve, if possible, the episcopal polity that they had inherited from the past for the sake of ordering the church (*Confessio Augustana*, 28; Apology, 14.1). In contemporary practice, some Lutheran churches have "one three-fold ministry," while others do not (*Episcopal Ministry* [also called the Lund Statement], §39). Questions of order remain intensely discussed, but without the expectation of a single proper form: "This cannot be construed on the basis of a principle, for the experiences the church has undergone play a decisive role" (*Apostolicity*, §265).

25 Catholics and Lutherans agree that the ministry is exercised both locally in the congregation and regionally. Both accept that the distinction between local and regional offices in the churches is more than the result of purely historical and human developments, or a matter of sociological necessity, but is the action of the Spirit. Furthermore, the differentiation of the ministry into a more local and a more regional office arises of necessity out of the intention and task of ministry to be a ministry of unity in faith.

In 1981, the second phase of international Lutheran–Catholic dialogue concluded its examination of the distinction between bishop and pastor with a cautious statement: "*If* both churches acknowledge that for faith this historical development of the one apostolic ministry into a more local and a more regional ministry has taken place with the help of the Holy Spirit and to this degree constitutes something essential for the church, then a *high degree* of agreement has been reached" (*Ministry*, §49; emphasis original). In 2006, the fourth phase cited this statement to show the advance that its own work had helped to achieve: "When one considers what has been shown above about the objective necessity of a differentiation within ministerial office, which is effectively present in the Lutheran churches and is recognized as such, then the hypothetical wording of this sentence can be changed into an affirmation" (*Apostolicity*, §280; see also *Church as Koinonia of Salvation*, §88, which includes the same quotation). Now "Catholics and Lutherans say together that the *episkope* of ministry must be exercised at two different levels, that is, both locally in the congregation and regionally" (*Apostolicity*, §280).

The fittingness and necessity of this differentiation is described by *Apostolicity* when it speaks of it as "arising out of the intention and task of the ministry to be a ministry of unity in faith." In "the congregation gathered for worship is the place where human beings hear and receive the word of God by word and sacrament. . . . But there are many such congregations. . . . In order that they may be one in faith in the one gospel and have communion with each other, there must be a ministry which takes responsibility for this unity" (§279; cf. *Church as Koinonia of Salvation*, §94).

In contemporary understanding, the practice of early Lutherans needs to be interpreted within its historical context, which was a time when the reformers "could not perceive or experience the office of bishop as an office of unity in faith." Furthermore, the fact that the early Lutherans practiced presbyteral ordination does not mean that they were without *episkope* or oversight. Their resort to presbyteral ordination, practiced "precisely because they held ministerial office to be essential for the existence of the church," did not remove their desire to maintain, as far as possible, their continuity with the practices of the whole church (*Apostolicity*, §282; cf. CA 28). In practice, "Lutheran churches too have always been episcopally ordered in the sense of having a ministry which bears responsibility for the communion in faith of individual congregations." While almost always recognizing a ministry of oversight, Lutherans nevertheless express this ministry through a variety of structures; "the supra-local ministry of oversight in Lutheran churches today is carried out both by individuals and by synods in which both the ordained and non-ordained work together" (*Apostolicity*, §279).

Lutherans continue to discuss the structure and roles of ministries of oversight. Some Lutheran churches have always maintained a historic episcopate. Thus, in Sweden, for example, the Catholic and Lutheran Dialogue Group has been able to make a common statement, "Concerning the Office of Bishop" (*Justification in the Life of the Church*, §300). In the United States, the Evangelical Lutheran Church in America committed itself in 1999 to share with the Episcopal Church "an episcopal succession that is both evangelical and historic" (*Called to Common Mission*, §12).[25] Other Lutheran churches use other designations for those exercising *episkope* (ephorus, synodal pastor, church president, etc.). It is important in Lutheran tradition to allow room for some diversity in the structures of *episkope*. Thus, the 2006 LWF Lund Statement says that it is "consistent with Lutheran understandings of the church" to develop "various synodical and collegial structures, which include the participation of both lay and ordained persons, and in which the episcopal ministry has a clearly defined role" (§50). Yet this document also affirmed that "the presence and exercise of a special ministry of oversight is consistent with the confessional character of Lutheran churches" and commended consideration of its "personal, collegial, and communal dimensions" (§2, 4). In all the work of oversight, there is "particular responsibility to care for the apostolic faithfulness and the unity of the church at large." This responsibility for unity calls for "substantial collegial relations with colleagues in the episkopé of other churches, particularly in the same region of the world" and for "cooperation with the wider Christian community" (*Episcopal Ministry*, §46–9).

---

25. Lutheran conversations with Anglicans have produced a number of agreements on the theology and practice of episcopal ministry, beginning with the 1987 *Niagara Report* and continuing with the 1993 *Porvoo Common Statement by the British and Irish Anglican Churches and Nordic and Baltic Lutheran Churches* and the 2001 *Waterloo Declaration by the Anglican Church of Canada and the Evangelical Lutheran Church in Canada*. For the reliance of this discussion on the Lutheran–Catholic dialogue, especially on ministry, for understanding apostolic succession, see the *Niagara Report* §3.

26 Catholics and Lutherans affirm together that all ministry, to the degree that it serves the *koinonia* of salvation, also serves the unity of the worldwide church and together we long for more complete realization of this unity.

In affirming that "all ordained ministers are commissioned to serve the unity and catholicity of the church," Lutherans have described the unity for which they yearn: "The communion that we seek ecumenically is made visible in shared forms of proclamation, which include participation in the one baptism and the one eucharist, and which is upheld by a mutually reconciled ministry. This communion in the means of grace witnesses to the healing and uniting power of the Triune God amidst the divisions of humankind, and represents the global communion of the universal church" (Lund Statement §54).

For Catholics, the bishop of Rome, successor of Peter, has a unique responsibility as pastor and teacher to this universal church (*Church as Koinonia of Salvation,* §70). He bears the responsibility for ensuring the unity of all the churches (John Paul II, *Ut unum sint,* §94).

The Lutheran legacy includes an openness to a rightly exercised primacy (*Church as Koinonia of Salvation,* §73). Lutherans have expressed a number of cautions about how the need for such an office is described and how it is to be exercised. Nevertheless, as *The Ministry in the Church* declared, "the possibility begins to emerge that the Petrine office of the bishop of Rome need not be excluded by Lutherans as a visible sign of the unity of the church as a whole, 'insofar as [this office] is subordinated to the primacy of the gospel by theological reinterpretation and practical restructuring'" (*Ministry,* §73 citing *Malta Report,* §66).

C. Eucharist

As stated above in this *Declaration*, in No. 6, Lutherans and Catholics agree on the mediating role of the "means of grace" by which God communicates to believers the benefits of Christ's redemptive and renewing work. By the gospel word and the sacraments, God's own power and influence envelop the believer's whole life through forgiveness of sins, union with the risen Christ, and sanctification by the Holy Spirit.

Among the sacraments, the eucharist or Lord's supper (1 Corinthians 11:20) is unique both in its benefits and in the various dimensions of its celebration: as memorial of Christ's death for our salvation, as encounter with him graciously giving forgiveness and nourishment, and as the pledge received of resurrection and glory to come.[26] Sadly, however, differences and even polemics over the eucharistic gift and event have divided Lutherans and Catholics both in their doctrine concerning this sacrament and, more painfully, in their separation, rather than communion, in celebrating and receiving this central blessing of God.

However, the past half century of our dialogues has brought to light hitherto unsuspected agreements between Lutherans and Catholics regarding the Lord's supper or eucharist. The following six agreements begin with our long-standing catechetical insistence on the spiritual benefits of eucharistic communion

---

26. St. Thomas Aquinas introduces the sacraments as involving "three times," that is, as commemorative signs of Christ's saving passion, as demonstrative signs of grace given by his passion, and as anticipatory signs of glory to come (*signum rememorativum, demonstrativum, praenuntiativum*). *Summa theologiae*, III, 60, 3. In his *Small Catechism*, Martin Luther instructs one to attend especially to the present gift of grace: "The words 'given for you' and 'shed for you for the forgiveness of sins' show us that forgiveness of sin, life, and salvation are given to us in the sacrament through these words, because where there is forgiveness of sin, there is also life and salvation" (*BC*, 362).

with Christ by reception of his body and blood (1). Then follow accounts of shared convictions gained by Catholics and Lutherans from 20th-century liturgical and theological study, such as the Trinitarian matrix and dynamic of celebrating the Lord's supper (2); the memorial (*anamnesis*) of Christ's once-for-all sacrifice in which he offered himself unto death for our salvation (3); the special mode, among other ways of Christ's presence, in which his body and blood are present and shared sacramentally (4); the future orientation of our celebration toward our Lord's return, with Holy Communion's promise of the risen life and heavenly banquet to come (5); and, finally, the personal and ecclesial communion (*koinonia*) realized among those who share in the body and blood of Christ, for "we, though many, are one body, for we all partake of the one bread" (1 Corinthians 10:17) (6).

27 Lutherans and Catholics agree in esteeming highly the spiritual benefits of union with the risen Christ given to them as they receive his body and blood in Holy Communion.

Catholics and Lutherans agree that when we receive the Lord's supper we are personally united with Christ. Receiving this gift is a source of great blessings for those who receive it in faith.

In explaining the Lord's supper in the *Large Catechism* (1529), Martin Luther taught a doctrine that became deeply formative of Lutheran faith and piety, that is, when he treated the "power and benefit, for which purpose the sacrament was really instituted. . . . This is clear and easily understood from the words . . . 'This is my body and blood, given and poured out FOR YOU for the forgiveness of sins.' That is to say, in brief, that we go to the sacrament because there we receive a great treasure, through and in which we obtain the forgiveness of sins. Why? Because the words are there, and they impart it to us! For this reason he bids me eat and drink, that it may be mine and do me good as a sure pledge and sign—indeed as the very gift he has provided for me against my sins, death, and all evils. Therefore it is appropriately called food of the soul . . . for it nourishes and strengthens the new creature."[27]

Less than 40 years later, the *Catechism of the Council of Trent* differed from Luther by assuming that communicants have received forgiveness of serious sins by confession and sacramental absolution, but it also taught, with comparable emphasis, the exalted benefits of receiving Christ the Lord in Holy Communion. The eucharist is "the fountain of all graces, containing as it does, in an admirable manner, the fountain itself of heavenly gifts and graces . . . Christ our Lord." On the imparting of grace: "If then, 'grace and truth came through Jesus Christ' (John 1:17), they must surely be poured into the soul which receives with purity and holiness him who said of himself, 'Those who eat my flesh and drink my blood abide in me, and I in them' (John 6:56)." Eucharistic communion, furthermore, cancels lesser faults, strengthens one against temptation, and, while giving peace of conscience in this life, also invigorates believers for their passage into unfading glory and beatitude with God.[28]

In our era, the world-level Lutheran–Catholic dialogue on the eucharist gave an agreed account of the sacrament's benefits, as

---

27. *BC*, 468–69. Another Lutheran confession, *The Smalcald Articles*, places the Sacrament of the Altar among the main forms in which the gospel is enunciated to believers—to be believed! Part III, art. 4, "Concerning the Gospel" (*BC*, 319).

28. *Catechism of the Council of Trent* for Parish Priests, trans. John A. McHugh and Charles J. Callan, 16th printing (New York: Joseph F. Wagner and London: B. Herder, 1934), 242–44. *The Catechism of the Catholic Church* (1992) updates this instruction on "The Fruits of Holy Communion," in §§1391–95 and §1416 ("In Brief").

believers are brought in a special way to be "in Christ": "Under the signs of bread and wine the Lord offers as nourishment his body and blood, that is himself, which he has given for all. He thus shows himself to be the 'living bread that came down from heaven' (John 6:51). When a believer receives this food in faith, he will be taken into a communion with Christ which is akin to the communion of the Son and the Father: 'Just as the living Father sent me, and I live because of the Father, so whoever eats me will live because of me' (John 6:57). Christ wills to be in us, and we are enabled to be in Christ: 'Those who eat my flesh and drink my blood abide in me and I in them' (John 6:56). This communion is rooted in eternity and reaches out again beyond time into eternity. 'The one who eats this bread will live forever'" (John 6:58).[29]

In 2010 the Roman Catholic–Lutheran Dialogue in Sweden and Finland related Holy Communion to baptism and then expressed the churches' high estimation of the eucharist by stating, "There is a particularly close link between baptism and the Eucharist, the Holy Mass, or Holy Communion. Both the

---

29. Lutheran–Roman Catholic Joint Commission, *The Eucharist* (Geneva: Lutheran World Federation, 1980; in German as *Das Herrenmahl*, 1978), §19. Among "supplementary studies," *The Eucharist* includes Harding Meyer's account of how Luther took the words of consecration as proclaiming salvation, even as *summa et compendium evangelii*, by which members of the congregation receive in faith the spiritual food offered them. In spite of this appendix, Albrecht Peters published a Lutheran critique of *The Eucharist* because it neglects themes central to Lutheran piety of the Lord's supper. Absent are, e.g., Luther's paralleling of the words of institution addressing forgiveness to the believer with other divinely mandated words of baptism and absolution from sin and the personal presence of the crucified and risen Lord who gives to communicants participation in his sacrificed and risen body ("Einheit im Herrenmahl?" *Theologische Revue* 75 [1979], 181–90). A wider presence of such misgivings came to light in several Lutheran churches' responses to *BEM* on the eucharist. See Martin Seils's study of these responses in *Lutheran Convergence?* LWF Report 25 (Geneva: LWF, 1988). However, it must be asked whether these Lutheran emphases, brought out in criticism of *The Eucharist*, should not be appreciated by Catholics as an enrichment of their eucharistic instruction and spirituality.

individual person and the church gain their spiritual life and strength from the Eucharist. Participation in Mass is the basic format for living as a Christian. Baptism incorporates the person who is baptized into the body of Christ and the Eucharist helps him or her to mature and grow therein. . . . Catholics and Lutherans profess together that Jesus Christ is really present in Holy Communion in bread and wine and that he forgives the faithful baptized their sins. Communion unites us with Christ, gives us the grace of God, and strengthens our faith."[30]

The Lutheran–Catholic conversation on the eucharist thus takes as its starting-point our shared high regard for the treasure of spiritual riches given to believers by their reception of the body and blood of Christ in Holy Communion. In the Reformation era, this regard was expressed in the catechisms with differing emphases, which however did not eliminate important areas of agreement. This shared esteem has become evident in our recent dialogues, which also show that our churches are agreed on several other dimensions of the Lord's supper, which the following texts will relate.

28 Catholics and Lutherans agree that in eucharistic worship the church participates in a unique way in the life of the Trinity: In the power of the Holy Spirit, called down upon the gifts and the worshiping community, believers have access to the glorified flesh and blood of Christ the Son as our food, and are brought in union with him and with each other to the Father.

Eucharistic prayers, since the earliest Christian times, have a dynamically Trinitarian structure. The Christian doctrine of God as Trinity is the traditional framework for liturgical community prayer. Classically, eucharistic prayers are addressed to the

---

30. *Justification in the Life of the Church*, §§215–16, referencing the affirmation of eucharistic promotion of growth stated in §75 of *Communio Sanctorum*.

Father, commemorating Jesus' words and actions and invoking the Holy Spirit upon the gifts and the congregation. The international dialogue's 1993 statement, *Church and Justification*, states clearly this Trinitarian texture of the eucharist: "The celebration of the Lord's Supper draws believers into the presence and communion of the triune God through thanksgiving (*eucharistia*) to the Father, remembrance (*anamnesis*) of Christ, and invocation (*epiclesis*) of the Holy Spirit" (§69; see also §49, taken up in no. 1, above, of this *Declaration*). Lutherans have also highlighted the proclamation nature of the eucharist, especially the institution narrative.

The world-level Lutheran–Catholic commission's 1978 document, *The Eucharist*, asserts, "The union with Christ into which we are drawn in the Eucharist through the power of the Holy Spirit ultimately leads to the eternal Father" (§29).[31] Because through the invocation of the Holy Spirit Christ is present in the eucharistic action, both as offering himself to us and to the Father, our participation in his offering nourishes us and introduces us into the mysterious inner rhythm of the life of God.

The Eucharist of 1978 gave evidence of how Trinitarian prayer shapes Catholic and Lutheran eucharistic worship by joining to the commission's agreed statement a series of texts both of Catholic eucharistic prayers and of orders of service for Holy Communion then in use in Lutheran churches of Germany, the United States (Lutheran Church in America), France, Slovakia, and Sweden.[32] The 2006 *Evangelical Lutheran Worship*, commended for use in the Evangelical Lutheran Church

---

31. The central "Joint Witness" of this commission unfolds the main dynamics of eucharistic worship, in three sections, namely, "Through, with, and in Christ" (§§13–20), "In the Unity of the Holy Spirit" (§§14–28), and "Glorification of the Father" (§§29–37).

32. *The Eucharist*, 29–60.

in America and the Evangelical Lutheran Church in Canada, gives settings for the service of Holy Communion, in which "The Great Thanksgiving" moves from the presider's invitation to give thanks and praise, to the "Holy, Holy, Holy," through the institution narrative, the memorial of Christ who died, rose, and will come again, to the concluding doxology of all honor and glory to God, the Father, Son, and Holy Spirit.[33]

29 Catholics and Lutherans agree that eucharistic worship is the memorial (*anamnesis*) of Jesus Christ, present as the one crucified for us and risen, that is, in his sacrificial self-giving for us in his death and in his resurrection (Romans 4:25), to which the church responds with its sacrifice of praise and thanksgiving.

Both Catholics and Lutherans commemorate Jesus' death and resurrection liturgically as they celebrate the eucharistic memorial (*anamnēsis*).[34] This is not simply a collective mental act recalling a past event but an action transcending time, which allows the believer to enter the reality of what faith recognizes as the pivotal event in human history. The people of God, assembled in the liturgical celebration, receive in faith the proclamation of Scripture and join in celebrating again Jesus' eucharistic gift of himself. They share now in Christ's

---

33. *Evangelical Lutheran Worship* (Minneapolis: Augsburg Fortress, 2006), for example, pp. 107–9 (Setting One), 129–33 (Setting Two). However, both of these Settings offer an alternative, condensed, form that moves directly from the "Holy, Holy, Holy" to the institution narrative and then to the Lord's Prayer, without the Trinitarian doxology (pp. 108, 130). This follows the tradition in Martin Luther's Latin Mass (*Formula missae*, 1523) and German Mass (*Deutsche Messe*, 1526).

34. The notion of *anamnesis* comes from Jesus' mandate, "Do this *eis tēn emēn anamnēsin*" ("as my memorial"; 1 Corinthians 11:24–25, Luke 22:19). It became a centerpiece of 20th-century ecumenical discussion through works on the eucharist by Gregory Dix, F. J. Leenhardt, Max Thurian, and J. J. von Allmen.

sacrificial act of praise and thanks to the Father, at the last supper and on the cross; they join him who is risen to make eternal intercession for humanity. They offer themselves to the Father along with him, since they form, under his headship, what St. Augustine calls "the whole Christ."

Catholics see in *each* celebration of the eucharist our inclusion in the one saving sacrifice of Christ offered for us to the Father. Lutherans generally emphasize the *uniqueness* of Christ's sacrifice on the cross, as a once-and-for-all event, whose benefits are now shared in Holy Communion, while understanding the present celebration of the eucharist as the church's prayer of thanks and affirmation in response to his sacrifice. The traditional contrast is between the Catholic emphasis on the movement *ad Patrem* (to the Father) and the Lutheran emphasis on the movement *ad populum* (to the people). In light of ecumenical discussions and liturgical renewal, Catholics have grown in appreciation of the message proclaimed and grace announced to the people in the eucharist, while Lutherans have grown in appreciation and recognition that the prayer of the people, spoken by the minister, is directed to the Father.

Statements of national and international dialogue commissions have argued that these two traditions on the eucharist and the sacrifice of Christ are not necessarily exclusive of each other. The international Joint Commission's 1978 statement, *The Eucharist*, took over from the World Council of Church's Faith and Order Commission this basic affirmation: "Christ instituted the eucharist, sacrament of his body and blood with its focus on the cross and resurrection, as the *anamnesis* of the whole of God's reconciling action in him. Christ himself with all that he has accomplished for us and for all creation (in his incarnation, servanthood, ministry, teaching, suffering, sacrifice, resurrection, ascension, and Pentecost) is present in this

anamnesis as is also the foretaste of his *Parousia* and the fulfil-
ment of the Kingdom" (§17).[35]

Regarding eucharistic sacrifice, *The Eucharist* explains: "The
notion of memorial, as understood in the Passover celebration
at the time of Christ—i.e., the making effective in the present of an event in the past—has opened the way to a clearer
understanding of the relationship between Christ's sacrifice
and the eucharist. In the *memorial celebration of the people of God*,
more happens than that past events are brought to mind by
the power of recall and imagination. The decisive point is not
that what is past is called to mind, but that the Lord calls his
people into his presence and confronts them with his salvation. In this creative act of God, the salvation event from the
past becomes the offer of salvation for the present and the
promise of salvation for the future. . . . In receiving in faith,
they are taken as his body into the reconciling sacrifice which
equips them for self-giving (Romans 12:1) and enables them
'through Jesus Christ' to offer 'spiritual sacrifices' in service to
the world (1 Peter 2:5). Thus is rehearsed in the Lord's supper
what is practiced in the whole Christian life" (§36).

The international commission, in *The Eucharist* (1978), affirmed
the agreement in this way: "Our two traditions agree in understanding the Eucharist as a *sacrifice of praise*. This is neither simple
verbal praise of God, nor is it a supplement or a complement
which the people from their own power add to the offering of

---

35. *The Eucharist* cites here the "Accra text" (1974), which was revised in *BEM*
of 1982. In *BEM-E* revisions occurred to give the following in place of the first
sentence cited above, "The eucharist is the memorial of the crucified and risen
Christ, i.e., the living and effective sign of his sacrifice, accomplished once and
for all on the cross and still operative on behalf of all humankind. The biblical
idea of memorial as applied to the eucharist refers to this present efficacy of
God's work when it is celebrated by God's people in a liturgy" (§5). The second
sentence cited above is in *BEM-E*, but with a revision which specifies that Christ
is present in the *anamnesis* as "granting us communion with himself" (§6).

praise and thanksgiving which Christ has made to the Father. The Eucharistic sacrifice of praise has only become possible through the sacrifice of Christ on the cross: therefore this remains the main content of the church's sacrifice of praise" (§37).

The Swedish-Finnish Lutheran–Catholic dialogue statement of 2010 adopts a wide framework in its section 4.5.1.3 on "The Eucharist as Thanksgiving, Remembrance, and Sacrifice" (§§222–31). A central statement on sacrifice moves from the Lutheran viewpoint to offer a context, both for what has been cited above from *The Eucharist* and for making important agreements explicit:

> Both Catholics and Lutherans emphasize the character of the Eucharist as a gift in return, since it is a thanksgiving sacrifice. The Lutheran Confessions . . . make a distinction between two kinds of offering, namely, sacrament (*sacramentum*) and sacrifice (*sacrificium*). The sacrament is God's gift of reconciliation and redemption, which comes first and which is given to us as a gift, while the sacrifice is the church's sacrifice of praise (*sacrificium laudis*), our response to God's gift. The response includes in the wider sense all good deeds that spring from faith. In the more narrow sense, this Eucharistic sacrifice includes the proclamation of the gospel, the profession of faith, prayer and thanksgiving, something that takes place at Mass.[36] In that sense the Mass as a whole can be seen as sacrifice, in which Christ first gives himself and his forgiveness to us and we respond by giving ourselves in thanksgiving to him. When the reformers criticized the medieval teaching about the sacrifice of the Mass, they were afraid that

---

36. At this point a note references the Apology of the Augsburg Confession, art. XXIV, §§17–26; *BC*, 260–63.

these two aspects would be confused so that the view of the sacrament as God's free gift would be dissolved and the Mass would be perceived as a human work, performed in order to satisfy God. However, if we seek to recover the sacramental meaning of the Eucharist, i.e. to understand it as a sacramental form, of which the content is the unique sacrifice of Christ, then the prerequisites exist for solving this controversial issue. (§229)

30 Lutherans and Catholics agree that in the sacrament of the Lord's supper, Jesus Christ himself is present: He is present truly, substantially, as a person, and he is present in his entirety, as Son of God and a human being.

Catholics conceive of this presence of Christ as being brought about through the *transformation* of the original substances or central realities of the eucharistic bread and wine into the substance or reality of the divinized body and blood of Christ by what Thomas Aquinas and the Council of Trent refer to as "transubstantiation."[37] Lutherans traditionally affirm that Christ is truly present *"in, with, and under"* the bread and wine, but do not usually speak of a transformation of the elements themselves.[38]

---

37. This terminology emerged in theological arguments against Berengar of Tours (d. 1088), who affirmed the Real Presence but denied any change in the elements. In 1079, a Council held in Rome required Berengar to profess and teach the "substantial conversion" of the elements (DH 700). In 13th-century scholastic theology, Aristotelian metaphysics of substance and accidents entered explanatory treatments of the Real Presence. Trent's teaching on the Real Presence in 1551 affirmed as doctrine the *conversio* of the substance of the elements into Christ's body and blood, adding that the church finds it fitting and proper to call this "transubstantiation" (DH 1642; see also *Catechism of the Catholic Church*, §1376, which comes after citations of Saints John Chrysostom and Ambrose).

38. Some recent Lutheran statements have drawn an analogy between the hypostatic union in Jesus of two natures, which continue to remain distinct, and the "sacramental union" of natural bread and wine with the person of the risen Lord in the eucharist, in which union does not involve mixture or change.

In Zürich, the Swiss reformer Ulrich Zwingli began teaching in 1525 that Christ's ascension ended his bodily presence among us and that the elements and actions of the supper only represent Christ for our commemorative spiritual eating in faith regarding Christ's death for us. Luther reacted vigorously in treatises defending the real presence.[39] In the *Large Catechism* (1529), he taught that the word of Christ, remembered and spoken over the eucharistic elements, "makes this a sacrament and distinguishes it from ordinary bread and wine, so that it is called and truly is Christ's body and blood."[40]

In 1530 the Augsburg Confession stated, "Concerning the Lord's Supper it is taught that the true body and blood of Christ are truly present under the form (*Gestalt*) of bread and wine in the Lord's Supper and are distributed and received there."[41] In response to the Confession, the *Confutation*, composed by Catholic theologians under direction of the Papal Legate and presented in the name of Emperor Charles V, stated, "The words of the tenth article contain nothing that would give cause for offense. They confess that the body and blood of Christ are truly and substantially present in the sacrament after the words of consecration."[42]

See Orthodox-Lutheran Joint Commission (2006), §4a; and *Justification in the Life of the Church*: Catholic–Lutheran Dialogue for Sweden and Finland (2010), §233. But in his conversation with Zwingli at Marburg in 1529, Luther insisted that the sacramental union between bread and Christ's body and the wine and Christ's blood is different from the hypostatic union of natures in Christ, observing that "this is not a personal union" (*LW* 37, 299ff.).

39. See, for example, *That These Words of Christ, "This is my Body," Still Stand Firm against the Fanatics* (1527), in *LW* 37, 13–150; and *Confession Concerning Christ's Supper* (1528), in *LW* 37, 161–372.

40. *BC*, 468. Luther's catechisms of 1529 are confessional documents of the Lutheran tradition.

41. Article X of the Confession, which adds against Zwingli and others, "Rejected, therefore, is also the contrary teaching." *BC*, 44.

42. *The Confutation of the Augsburg Confession*, given in *Sources and Contexts of The Book of Concord*, eds. Robert Kolb and James A. Nestingen (Minneapolis: Fortress,

Although controversy made necessary a shift of attention to the objective reality of Christ's presence, Luther's catechetical texts cited in No. 1, above, are an emphatic teaching on the saving and reconciling Christ being present and active as he gives his body and blood, with its blessings and benefits, in the Lord's supper or eucharistic celebration.

Both traditional Catholic and traditional Lutheran approaches, then, different as they are in expression, affirm Christ's real, substantial presence in the sacrament. In the faith of both churches, when one receives the eucharistic elements or species, one truly receives the body and blood of Christ in a sacramental way, and so comes into communion with Christ, in order to be on pilgrimage with him.

The 1978 statement of the international Joint Commission, *The Eucharist*, draws this conclusion about the different ways Catholics and Lutherans traditionally conceive of eucharistic presence:

> The ecumenical discussion has shown that these two positions must no longer be regarded as opposed in a way that leads to separation. The Lutheran position affirms the Catholic tradition that the consecrated elements do not simply remain bread and wine, but rather, by the power of the creative word, are given as the body and blood of Christ. In this sense Lutherans also occasionally speak, as does the Greek tradition, of a "change." The concept of transubstantiation, for its part, is intended as a confession and preservation of the Mystery-character of the Eucharistic presence; it is not intended as an explanation of *how* this change occurs. (§51)

2001), 112. Consequently, Melanchthon's Apology of the Augsburg Confession, treats art. X briefly, while adding texts from Greek Fathers to show "that we defend the position received in the entire church. . . . Moreover, we are talking about the presence of the living Christ, for we know that death no longer has dominion over him (Romans 6:9)." *BC*, 185.

31 Catholics and Lutherans agree that eucharistic communion, as sacramental participation in the glorified body and blood of Christ, is a pledge that our life in Christ will be eternal, our bodies will rise, and the present world is destined for transformation, in the hope of uniting us in communion with the saints of all ages now with Christ in heaven.

As a sharing in the life of Father, Son, and Holy Spirit, the eucharist directs the gaze of the assembled ecclesial body on the future, when history will be endlessly fulfilled by our sharing in the divine Mystery. As the 1993 document *Church and Justification* put it, "[The Church] is already a partaking in the *koinonia* of the Father, Son and Holy Spirit; but as the pilgrim Church, it is such provisionally and in fragmentary fashion; and this means in anticipation and expectation of its final destination, which is still pending: consummation in the Kingdom of God, in which the triune God will be 'all in all' (1 Corinthians 15:24–28)" (§73).[43]

The International Commission's statement, *The Eucharist*, emphasized this:

> The form and effect of the Eucharist are a promise of the eternal glory to which we are destined, and a sign pointing to the new heaven and new earth towards which we are moving: that is why the Eucharist directs our thoughts to the Lord's coming, and brings it near to us. It is a joyful anticipation of the heavenly banquet, when redemption shall be fully accomplished and all creation shall be delivered from bondage. . . . The Lord's Supper enables us to understand the future glory as the boundless and eternal wedding feast to which we are invited by the Lord. As a fraternal meal, in which Christ frees and unites, it turns our

---

43. See statement No. 11 above, in the Church section.

gaze to the promised eternal kingdom of unlimited freedom and righteousness. (§§43–44; cf. §70)

In *Church and Justification* (1993) the Commission is more explicit still about the relation of the eucharistic liturgy to the Christian dead:

> Catholics and Lutherans confess in common that the "communion of saints" is the community of those united in sharing in the word and sacraments (the *sancta*) in faith, through the Holy Spirit: the community of "those who are sanctified in Christ Jesus [and] called to be saints [the *sancti*]" (1 Corinthians 1:2). In the Lutheran Confessions, too, there is a fundamental adherence to the idea of a living communion with the saints, for despite criticism of invocation of the saints, it is not denied that we should give "honor to the saints": in thanks to God for their gifts of grace, in the strengthening of our faith because of their example, and in "imitation, first of their faith and then of their other virtues, which each should imitate in accordance with his calling" (Apology 21.4–7; *Book of Concord* 229–30). . . . Vatican II placed the ideas of the fathers and the practice of venerating the saints in an ecclesiological context (*Lumen Gentium* §§50–51). It stresses the eschatological character of the Church as the pilgrim people of God, and speaks of that people's "union with the Church in heaven" (*LG* 50). (§§293–94)[44]

---

44. The U.S. dialogue report, *Hope of Eternal Life: Lutherans and Catholics in Dialogue XI* (2011), says: "This intimate communion in the Spirit is not broken by death. As the Catholics and Lutherans stated in an earlier round: 'The fellowship of those sanctified, the "holy ones" or saints, includes believers both living and dead. There is thus a solidarity of the church throughout the world with the church triumphant.' This solidarity across the barrier of death is particularly evident in the Eucharist, which is always celebrated in unity with the hosts of heaven" (§217, quoting *Lutherans and Catholics in Dialogue VIII: The One Mediator, the Saints, and Mary*, eds. H. George Anderson, J. Frances Stafford, and Joseph A. Burgess [Minneapolis: Augsburg, 1992], §103).

32 Lutherans and Catholics agree that sharing in the celebration of the eucharist is an essential sign of the unity
of the church, and that the reality of the church as a community
is realized and furthered sacramentally in the eucharistic celebration. The eucharist both mirrors and builds the church in
its unity.

The church is united, above all, by communion in the life and
the supernatural gifts of God. This unity cannot be separated
from unity in the confession of faith; it also cannot be separated from a lived unity or fellowship among Christians, and
it is rooted in the "one baptism" by which all Christians are
made members of the body of Christ. But the eucharist has
a unique relevance for showing forth and building up the
church of Jesus Christ.

The 1978 statement, *The Eucharist*, states that the unity of
individual disciples with the Lord, and the unity of the whole
church, which is his body, is rooted in and fed by the celebration of the eucharist: "Under the signs of bread and wine the
Lord offers as nourishment his body and blood, that is himself, which he has given for all. . . . In giving himself, Christ
unites all who partake at his table: the many become 'one
body' (1 Corinthians 10:17). In the power of the Holy Spirit,
they are built up as the one people of God. 'It is the Spirit that
gives life' (John 6:63). The eucharistic meal is thus the source
of the daily new life of the people of God, who through it are
gathered together and kept in one faith" (§§19–20).

Pointing to the sacramental roots of the communion among
believers in faith and in Christian practice, the 1993 statement, *Church and Justification*, declared: "In a special way the
[eucharistic] celebration is the *koinonia* of believers with the

crucified and risen Lord present in the Supper, and for that reason it also creates and strengthens the *koinonia* of the faithful among and with each other" (§69; cf. §57).

The Swedish-Finnish dialogue gave in 2010 an account of eucharist and church unity, in which the commission proceeded from very basic aspects to draw on Augustine's interpretation of key Pauline texts:

> The Eucharist, or Holy Communion, is already by definition a public or a communal event. Jesus Christ unites all those who partake of his body and blood. Holy Communion thus expresses and strengthens the spiritual communion that exists between Christ and the individual Christian, between the church and its members, and between different local churches. Those who share the common bread and wine should profess their common faith and share all their joy and all their suffering with one another. As members of the body of Christ, we become participants of the life of Christ as well as of the life of one another (1 Corinthians 12:27). The Church Father St. Augustine exhorts us to fellowship, which culminates in the Eucharist: "'Only one bread,' he [i.e., St. Paul] says. Regardless of the many breads that are distributed, it is still 'only one bread.' Regardless of how many breads remain on the altars of Christ across the whole earth, it is still 'only one bread.' But what is this 'one bread'? He expounds it in the shortest possible way, 'though many, we are only one body.' This bread, which is the body of Christ, the apostle calls the church: 'You are the body of Christ, and each one of you is its member.' What you receive, that you are, by grace, through which you are saved, and you confirm that

we are all one when you answer 'Amen.' It is, as you see, the sacrament of unity." (§220)[45]

The dialogue group concluded: "Catholics and Lutherans agree that Holy Communion is a celebration of solidarity" (§221). For this reason, our present inability to share eucharistic communion on a regular basis reveals all the more dramatically our ongoing need for fullness of unity in faith, practice, and, eventually, eucharistic sharing.

---

45. The Commission cited Augustine's Sermon 229A, giving the Latin original in note 106 of the document.

IV. Remaining Differences and Reconciling Considerations

This section moves beyond the 32 affirmations of the *Declaration* and its documentation to consider certain unresolved matters. This part of the *Declaration* treats 15 topics that have arisen from study of the dialogues in the three areas of church, ministry, and eucharist. The topics represent doctrinal differences of varying gravity. This part differs from the parts concerning the agreements (parts II and III) in having a more tentative character, which serves to make clear the "on the way" dynamic of the Lutheran–Roman Catholic ecclesial relationship. Our labors toward reconciliation are not yet finished, even after decades of dialogue. This section presents, but does not propose to treat in a complete manner, the Lutheran–Roman Catholic differences with divisive effects.

Like the preceding parts, this part also arises from the work of the dialogues. In places, the dialogue reports have presented issues of doctrinal difference that the dialogue had not resolved, but some of the issues raised do prove, after consideration, not to be church-dividing. Therefore, this part also shows positive benefits from the dialogues, going beyond the major agreements stated and documented in parts II and III.

A. Church

In addition to yielding the significant agreements articulated above in common affirmations, five decades of Lutheran–Catholic dialogues have also treated matters of substantial differences and firmly held points of contention regarding ecclesiology. In important matters the dialogues have discovered and set forth convincingly that Lutherans and Catholics do share common views. At times, each side has exaggerated the differences held by the other. In many cases, each side has grown in appreciation for the insights espoused by the other side. But the dialogues have also articulated situations of remaining differences not yet amenable to reconciliation. The following five examples strive to make clear both the progress made "on the way" to unity and the remaining differences that impede this journey.

1. DESIGNATING THE CHURCH: "CONGREGATION OF THE FAITH-FUL" OR "SACRAMENT OF SALVATION"

Lutherans define the church with emphasis on its reception of salvation, that is, as the assembly or congregation of the faithful (congregatio fidelium) *in which the gospel is taught purely and the sacraments administered rightly (CA VII and VIII).*[46] *Recent Catholic ecclesiology has brought to the fore the analogous use of the term* sacrament *for the church, describing the church as being "in Christ, a kind of sacrament or instrumental sign of intimate union with God and of the unity*

---

46. *Church and Justification*, §§109–12, sets forth the Lutheran position from Luther and the confessions, concluding, "The Church is therefore the *congregatio fidelium*, the congregation of salvation as a faith-congregation, founded by God's word and bound to it: 'God's Word cannot be present without God's people, and God's people cannot be without God's Word'" (§111, citing WA 50, 629).

of all humanity," or simply as "the universal sacrament of salvation" *(LG 1 and 48).*[47] *Lutherans register reservations regarding this Catholic terminology by insisting that sacraments are linked with Christ in his saving action toward the church.*[48] *The church does mediate salvation, but only as recipient, especially through the sacraments, of Christ's grace of salvation.*[49]

The traditional Lutheran designation of the church, "congregation of the faithful," emphasizes that the church comes

---

47. "Christ, when he was lifted up from the earth, drew all people to himself (see John 12:32 Greek text); rising from the dead (see Romans 6:9), he sent his life-giving Spirit down on his disciples and through the Spirit constituted his body which is the church as the universal sacrament of salvation" (*LG* 48). A more elaborated statement is in *Church and Justification,* §§120–24; a more concise account is *Communio Sanctorum,* §87. Designating the church as "sacrament" is one part of Vatican II's biblical and patristic replacement of the previously predominant social-institutional conception of the church, defended in early modern Catholic theology largely concerned with apologetical argumentation. In the renewal, "sacrament" is one theme among several, as shown by M. J. Le Guillou's sketch in the entry "Church" in *Sacramentum Mundi,* 6 vols., ed. Karl Rahner et al. (Freiburg: Herder, 1968–70), 1:318–23.

48. On this, CA XIII states the purposes of the sacraments "not only to be marks of profession among human beings but much more to be signs and testimonies of God's will toward us, intended to arouse and strengthen faith in those who use them" (*BC,* 47). CA XXV, on confession, explains with reference to absolution the structure of Lutheran sacramental administration and reception, for "people are taught to make the most of absolution because it is the voice of God and is pronounced following the command of God. The power of the keys is praised and remembered for bringing such great consolation to terrified consciences, both because God requires faith so that we believe that absolution is God's own voice resounding from heaven and because this faith truly obtains and receives the forgiveness of sins" (*BC,* §73). This account of absolution explains what is central to the dominical sacraments, that is, "the voice of God" spoken in Trinitarian consecration of those being baptized and in the words of eucharistic institution addressed to the worshiping congregation.

49. "The individual sacraments are means of salvation because through them Jesus Christ accomplishes salvation and thus establishes and preserves the church. This means that the church does not actualize its own existence in the sacraments; rather the church receives salvation and its very being from Christ and only as recipient does it mediate salvation. In this perspective, the individual sacraments are linked with Christ as he faces the church. One should be reticent about language which blurs this distinction." *Church and Justification,* §128; also, *Communio Sanctorum,* §88.

together as an assembly by receiving salvation given by God, while the Catholic designation "sacrament of salvation," used analogously (*Church and Justification*, §123), highlights the church's role, in Christ, as sign and instrument of salvation for its members and the world.

Catholics, however, do not deny the accuracy and significance of the term *congregatio fidelium* regarding the church. As the predominant definition for the church in medieval theology, it was the definition employed by the *Catechism of the Council of Trent.*[50] It appears as well in Vatican II and resonates with several themes of the Council.[51]

From these themes it follows: "The church lives as a communion of believers, not by its own strength but entirely from God's gift" (*Church and Justification*, §116).

Regarding the designation of the church as sacrament, Lutheran theology, while usually reserving the term *sacrament* for rites that are instituted by Christ, promise grace, and employ material elements, does share the central concern of Catholic sacramental ecclesiology, namely, that the church is indefectibly united to Christ, while remaining distinct from him as it carries out the signifying and instrumental role given to it. "As mediator of word and sacrament, the church is the instrument through which the Holy Spirit sanctifies; 'it is the mother that begets and bears every Christian through the Word of God'" (*Church and Justification*, §127, quoting Luther's Large Catechism I, 40ff.). As

---

50. *Catechism of the Council of Trent* I, 10, 2; I, 10, 5. See *Church and Justification*, §113.

51. *Church and Justification*, §§114–15, offers a cluster of texts, including designations of individual congregations as "congregations of the faithful" (*AG* §§15, 19, and *PO* §4), and affirms, "This communion with God and of human beings among themselves is brought about by God's word and the sacraments" (§114).

recipient of God's grace, mediated to believers by word and sacrament, the church also becomes an instrument of God's grace, which it administers through the preaching of the word and administration of the sacraments.[52]

Furthermore, the Swedish-Finnish Catholic–Lutheran dialogue (§144) expressed openness by Lutherans to using "sacrament" and "sacramental" to refer to the church: "Just as the Christ is called the original sacrament, so the church may be called the fundamental sacrament. This has been expounded thus: 'The church is not one more sacrament, but that sacramental framework, within which the other sacraments exist. Christ himself is present and active in the church. The church is therefore, both according to Roman-Catholic and Lutheran–Melanchthonian tradition, in a mysterious way an effective sign, something which by grace effects what it signifies.'"[53]

Considerations moving forward

Together with Lutherans, Catholics understand the church as "the assembly of faithful or saints which lives from God's word and the sacraments" (*Church and Justification*, §117). Although Lutherans and Catholics differ over use of the term *sacrament* to designate the church, they affirm together that the church is (1) both a creation of the word (*creatura verbi*) and servant of

---

52. "According to the Lutheran conception, the church is the community in which the God-ordained means of grace—word and sacrament—become effective to the people. Thus the church has, in a derived sense, the character of an instrument of salvation: as mediator of word and sacrament, it is the instrument through which the Holy Spirit makes people holy" (*Communio Sanctorum*, §88).

53. Quoting *Kyrkam som sacrament (The Church as Sacrament: A Report on Ecclesiology)*, published by the Church of Sweden Central Board and the Catholic Diocese of Stockholm, Uppsala—[Stockholm, 1999], 12. See also the Faith and Order document, *The Church: Towards a Common Vision* (2013), §27, proposing that, as explained, the differences of formulation on this point may remain as being compatible and mutually acceptable.

the word (*ministra verbi*) that it has received, (2) a sign for all people of the universal saving will of God, (3) an instrument of grace, by word and sacrament, (4) essentially shaped by both the reception of and administration of word and sacrament, and (5) constantly subject to the Lord in its action through which God imparts salvation as his gift. "Where this is together taught, there is material agreement, even if different judgments exist about the analogous use of the term 'sacrament' in relationship to the church."[54]

2. THE CHURCH HOLY AND SINFUL

While Lutherans and Catholics both confess that the church on earth is holy, despite the presence and influence of sin at work in it, they set different limits in calling the church itself "holy" and "sinful," with Catholics refraining from calling the church itself "sinful," and Lutherans maintaining that no church office or decision is so immune from error and sin as to be exempt from critical examination in view of reform.

An extensive, profound, and convincing grounding of the church's God-given holiness is common to Lutherans and Catholics.[55] Especially from the early creeds' affirmation of holiness as a church attribute and from Christ's promise that his followers, united to him and guided by the Holy Spirit, will abide in the truth, Catholics distinguish the personal sinfulness of believers from the "indestructibility of the one holy

---

54. *Communio Sanctorum*, §89. In his ecclesiology text of 2011, W. Kasper devotes three pages to "sacrament" as a designation of the church. He presents several valuable ecclesiological considerations but concludes that the technical schemes adopted in this development show that the topic is ill suited for use in basic instruction of believers. *Katholische Kirche. Wesen—Wirklichkeit—Sendung* (Freiburg: Herder, 2011), 126–29.

55. *Church and Justification* tells in §§148–52 how the holiness of the church is rooted in the holiness of the triune God and in Christ's presence to his disciples "to the end of the age" (Matthew 28:20).

church," which cannot apostatize from God and become "sinful" in an ultimate sense (*Church and Justification*, §150, from *LG* 39; and §153, quoted).

Lutherans, for their part, hold that Catholics see the church's holiness objectivized in specific ecclesial offices and decisions, to which they attribute the Holy Spirit's aid in such a way that these offices and decisions are rendered immune from human error and sinfulness. From a Lutheran perspective, ecclesial offices and decisions are carried out by sinful human beings. Thus, they continue to be imperfect and can obscure the indestructible holiness of the church.[56] Lutherans believe that, in this present age, the power of evil and sin is at work in the church.

However, Catholics, while asserting that the church is holy in the ultimate sense, agree with Lutherans that the power of evil and sin is at work in it. The church of complete and perfect holiness will appear only at the end of its earthly pilgrimage. Catholics and Lutherans agree that the pilgrim church includes "wheat and weeds" (Matthew 13:38), that is, good and evil people along with true and false teachers. Catholics agree with CA VIII about the presence of "many false Christians, hypocrites, and even open sinners . . . among the godly" (*Church and Justification*, §§153–54). Consequently, believers are in need of daily repentance and the forgiveness of sins,

---

56. *Church and Justification*, §§160–162, for example, "Above all, this Lutheran query is directed at ecclesial offices and decisions which serve people's salvation and sanctification. The question arises when the Holy Spirit's aid is attributed to them in such a way that, as such, they appear to be immune from the human capacity for error and sinfulness and therefore from needing to be examined" (§161). Controversy arises over the Catholic beliefs (1) that revealed truth can be articulated in binding propositions and forms of expressing the gospel which are inerrant and infallible; (2) that there are abiding ecclesial offices which are willed by God's providence; and (3) that the saints sanctified by God are not all anonymous but can be named with certainty by canonization and addressed as those perfected. *Church and Justification*, §163.

and the church is in constant need of cleansing and renewal. After the passage in which Vatican II asserted that the Church of Christ subsists in the Catholic Church, there came this contrast: "While Christ 'holy, blameless, unstained' (Hebrews 7:26) knew no sin (see 2 Corinthians 5:21) and came only to expiate the sins of the people (see Hebrews 2:17), the church, containing sinners in its own bosom, is at one and the same time holy and always in need of purification (*sancta simul et purificanda*) and it pursues unceasingly penance and renewal" (*LG* 8). The church is marked by a "genuine though imperfect holiness" (*LG* 48).[57] The practice of ecumenism begins with church reform, for, "In its pilgrimage on earth, Christ summons the church to that continual reformation (*ad hanc perennem reformationem*), of which it is always in need, in so far as it is an institution of human beings on earth" (*UR* 6, cited in *Church and Justification*, §156).[58]

Lutherans, for their part, believe in the indestructibility and abiding existence of the church as the one holy people of God. "A Christian holy people is to be and to remain on earth until the end of the world. This is an article of faith that cannot be

---

57. *Lumen gentium*, §48, goes on to say that "until the arrival of the new heavens and new earth in which justice dwells (see 2 Pt 3:13), the pilgrim church in its sacraments and institutions, which belong to this age, carries the figure of this world which is passing and it dwells among creatures who groan and until now are in the pains of childbirth and await the revelation of the children of God (see Romans 8:19– 21)."

58. Examples of Catholic reforming action are the nine practice-oriented "decrees" of Vatican II, which lay down norms for the pastoral office of bishops, formation for priesthood, the ministry and life of priests, the lay apostolate, renewal of religious life, use of the mass media, the contribution of the Catholic Eastern Churches, the church's missionary activity, and the ecumenical orientation and action of the whole church. In the Dogmatic Constitution on Divine Revelation, *Dei Verbum*, the concluding ch. VI gives norms for renewed scripture usage in the church, while in the Constitution on the Liturgy, *Sacrosanctum Concilium*, only ch. I is doctrinal, while chs. II–VII prescribe reforms of liturgical practice.

terminated until that which it believes comes" (Luther, WA 50, 626; *LW* 41, 148). In this sense, the Augsburg Confession affirms "that one holy Christian church will be and will remain forever" (CA VII). This belief in the indestructibility of the one holy church includes the idea that in the ultimate sense the church cannot apostatize from the truth and fall into error. Thus, Lutherans confess, together with Catholics, that the church is "holy" and that this holiness is indestructible (*Church and Justification*, §§151–52, citing CA in 151).

Considerations moving forward

Though drawing different limits in usage of "holy" and "sinful" to characterize the state of the church on earth, Lutherans and Catholics together affirm the ultimate holiness of the church, a holiness deriving solely from union with the triune God, who alone is holy. At the same time, both sides observe that the church's members are engaged in an ongoing struggle against sin and error (*Church and Justification*, §§153–55). Thus, in this usage, Lutheran and Roman Catholic explications are, in their difference, largely open to one another.[59] However, the discussion in *Church and Justification* raised an issue of difference that was not resolved and will return below: the nature and limits of the binding character of church teaching.[60]

3. DOCTRINE ENUNCIATED IN AND BY THE CHURCH

Lutherans and Catholics agree that the church is authorized by God and empowered by the Holy Spirit to teach and to distinguish truth from error

---

59. *The Church: Towards a Common Vision* offers a similar explanation in §§35–36, concluding, "Holiness and sin relate to the life of the Church in different and unequal ways. Holiness expresses the Church's identity according to the will of God, while sin stands in contradiction to this identity (cf. Romans 6:1–11)."

60. See the discussion below of the fourth point of difference in ecclesiology.

(Church and Justification, §205). Like the church of every age, the Lutheran as well as the Roman Catholic Church has been "a teaching church which sees itself under the continuing commission to preserve the truth of the gospel and to reject error" (Church and Justification, *§207). Both sides agree that the church has the promise of the Holy Spirit, who leads it to truth. "The church does not have the truth at its disposal. It has the promise that it will remain in the truth if it allows itself constantly to be called back to it."*[61] *However, a difference surfaces over how this teaching ministry is exercised.*[62]

Catholics attribute a special responsibility and authority for teaching to the ministry and in particular to the episcopate; this position, however, does not constitute an essential difference from Lutheran doctrine and practice (*Church and Justification*, §208). But in viewing the Catholic Church, Lutheran reformers believed that the inerrancy promised to the whole church had been concentrated too fully in the teaching ministry of bishops and popes in such a manner that the primacy of the gospel was at stake (*Church and Justification*, §§210–11). Lutherans have feared the magisterium's "monopoly" over interpretation of Scripture in enunciation of doctrine (*Apostolicity*, §407).

However, Catholics do acknowledge a role and responsibility for the whole people of God, because the magisterium of bishops and the pope is anchored in the entire community's life of faith. The bishops' binding teaching office is exercised in fellowship and community with the whole people of God,

---

61. *Communio Sanctorum*, §43, correcting the English translation that omitted the all-important fourth word ("not") in sentence cited.

62. This was set forth at length in Round VI of the U.S. dialogue, on *Teaching Authority and Infallibility in the Church* (1978), in *Church and Justification*, §§205–22, and most recently in *The Apostolicity of the Church*, in §§376–89 ("The Ministry of Teaching in Lutheran Churches") and §§411–28 ("The Teaching Office in Catholic Doctrine").

where there is a many-sided exchange among church members, since all God's people are called to discover and witness to God's truth (*Church and Justification*, §216; *Ministry in the Church*, §51; *LG* 12). The pope's teaching office is exercised in collegiality with other bishops and in concert with the *sensus fidelium*.[63] Furthermore, in the teaching ministry, the magisterium is bound to the canon of Scripture and apostolic tradition (*Church and Justification*, §217; *DV* 10).

For their part, Lutherans have affirmed the church's continuing commission to preserve the truth of the gospel and to reject error. "Its catechisms, especially Luther's Large Catechism, and most particularly the Confessions with their 'teaching' and 'rejecting' exemplify this" (*Church and Justification*, §207). Lutherans historically have had a strong sense of the ecclesial teaching function of ministers and theological faculties, asserting that no one should teach publicly in the church without a proper call (CA XIV; *BC* 47). The Lutheran Confessions also acknowledge the teaching responsibility of bishops (CA 28, 21f). The churches of the Lutheran Reformation carry out binding teaching, subject to the primacy of the gospel, and they have instruments and organs for performing this ministry. The ordained ministry has specific responsibility for public teaching, and bishops have the task of public teaching at the supra-local level. At the global level, The Lutheran World Federation has exercised the role of judging doctrine, affirming ecumenical statements, and administering discipline (*Apostolicity*, §388).[64]

---

63. *The Apostolicity of the Church*, after presenting the teaching authority on the pope according to the two Vatican Councils, includes this point: "Vatican II's Dogmatic Constitution on the Church modifies the treatment of the hierarchy and papal infallibility by placing them within the witness given by the whole people of God in its prophetic role" (§419).

64. There has been ongoing discussion and debate among Lutherans regarding the role of The Lutheran World Federation (LWF) and the implications of its

Considerations moving forward

Both Lutherans and Catholics ascribe to the Holy Spirit the effective maintaining of the truth of the gospel and the correct celebration of the sacraments. The church is authorized by God and empowered by the Holy Spirit to distinguish truth from error through faithful teaching. Both affirm the need for a ministry and office of teaching, exercised within the whole church in concert with all the faithful. Lutherans and Catholics agree together that "in spite of their different configurations of teaching ministries . . . the church must designate members to serve the transmission of the gospel, which is necessary for saving faith" (*Apostolicity*, §453). Lutherans and Catholics agree that, for the church to abide in the truth, the teaching office must be present and functioning at local and regional levels (*Apostolicity*, §453).

4. THE NATURE AND LIMITS OF THE BINDING CHARACTER OF CHURCH TEACHING

For Catholics, the Lord's promise that the church will abide in the truth grounds a conviction that the episcopal and papal magisterium can articulate the truth of the gospel in doctrinal affirmations that express or interpret divine revelation. Because of the mandate and

---

decision to become not only a federation but a "communion" of churches. These milestones are clearly important. While still a "federation" only, the LWF exercised discipline at its Seventh Assembly in Budapest in 1984, suspending two Southern African churches due to their continued failure to end racial division in their churches. The LWF has exercised a role in judging dogma by its formal reception of the *Joint Declaration on the Doctrine of Justification* (1999). Other LWF communion-defining actions included a 2010 formal apology to the Mennonite community for the legacies of past persecution of Anabaptists as well as commitments "to interpret the Lutheran Confessions in light of the jointly described history between Lutherans and Anabaptists and to take care that this action of the LWF will bear fruit in the teaching of the Lutheran Confessions in the seminaries and other educational activities of our member churches" (Eleventh Assembly, Stuttgart, 2010; www.lwf-assembly.org/uploads/media/Mennonite-Statement-En_03.pdf).

authority of bearers of this office, the faithful are obliged to accept their teaching with a "religiously based assent" (eique religioso animi obsequio adhaerere debent).[65] *Such teaching may in certain cases even be inerrant and infallible, and thus bind church members to assent at this level* (Church and Justification, §163; Communio Sanctorum, §65). *Lutherans see the church's ministry and decisions as liable to error and so hold that as a matter of principle they must be open to examination by the whole people of God. Believers have the right and duty to consult Scripture in order "to test whether the proclamation offered to them accords with the gospel."[66] Consequently, any teaching claiming to be binding must be met with a reservation* (Vorbehalt) *regarding its binding nature.*

In Lutheran understanding, the church fulfills its responsibility for articulating doctrine through "a many-layered process, aiming for consensus through the participation of various responsibility-bearers," such as bishops, theological teachers, pastors, and congregations. The ordained and nonordained cooperate in seeking a comprehensive agreement that will prove itself as continuous with the preaching and teaching tradition of the church. All members of the church, according to their respective callings, take part in the responsibility of teaching.[67]

Critically, Lutherans hold that the gospel cannot without reservation be consigned to an ecclesiastical ministry for its expression and preservation. Such a ministry is carried out by human beings liable to err. But error must not take on binding force in the church. Such a ministry must not claim the

---

65. *Communio Sanctorum*, §65, citing a phrase from *Lumen gentium*, 25, with its intricate account of the episcopal and papal magisterium, on the one hand, and of the corresponding types of adherence called for by the faithful.

66. *Communio Sanctorum*, §66, citing the *Lehrordnung der VELKD von 16.6.1956*, ed. Martin Lindow (Hanover 1989).

67. *Communio Sanctorum*, §66, based on the *Lehrordnung der VELKD von 16.6.1956*, ed. Martin Lindow (Hanover 1989).

sovereignty and ultimate binding force that is reserved to the gospel alone. What officeholders teach in the church must be ultimately measured against the gospel to make sure that believers are relying on God's words and not human words (*Church and Justification*, §212).[68]

A statement of this Lutheran conviction came in *Church and Justification*:

> For the sake of the gospel, the Reformation doctrine of justification therefore requires that the church's ministry and its decisions should as a matter of principle be open to examination by the whole people of God. As a matter of principle justification debars them from insulating themselves from such an examination. In regard to its decisions, the teaching ministry must permit "question or censure," as the Apology says, by the church as a whole, for which the promise of abiding in the truth holds good, and which is the people of God, the body of Christ, and the temple of the Holy Spirit. Otherwise it seems doubtful from a Reformation perspective that the teaching ministry serves the word of God and is not above it. (*Church and Justification*, §213)[69]

Communio Sanctorum speaks of doctrinal decisions being tested against Holy Scripture, which Lutherans believe to have in

---

68. Similarly: "Doctrinal decisions are dependent on recognition by the congregations (reception) and are fundamentally open to testing against Holy Scripture. The maintenance of the church in the truth is here 'not bound to a certain process or to an always pre-existing authority.'" *Communio Sanctorum*, §67, citing *Kirchliches Leben in ökumenischer Verpflichtung*, ed. Hermann Brandt (Stuttgart: Calver Verlag, 1989), 133.

69. This cites the Apology, Arts. 7 and 8, no. 23, giving what the Catholic opponents seem to hold, namely, the Roman pontiff's unlimited power, "which no one is allowed to question or censure" BC 178. The final sentence alludes to Vatican II's *Dei Verbum* where it claims that the magisterium is not above the word of God but stands at its service (no. 10).

itself, based on God's promise, the power to present the truth of God effectively and to interpret itself (*Communio Sanctorum*, §68). When the teaching ministry respects this reservation regarding binding teaching, this is the respect due to the independence and ultimate binding nature of the gospel and the grace of God (*Church and Justification*, §214).

The Lutheran position set forth in *Church and Justification* prompted a Catholic statement extending from the inerrancy in faith of the faithful as a whole to the conviction that the apostolic tradition develops in the church amid its many-sided life with the help of the Holy Spirit (*Church and Justification*, §§216–21).[70] In doctrinal development, previous teachings come to be reformulated and reconfigured, in a painstaking quest for the truth, in which the faithful, bishops, and theologians participate (*Church and Justification*, §221).[71] But in officially transmitting both traditional and newly developed Catholic doctrine, the bishops, in communion with the bishop of Rome, are authentic teachers of the faith by virtue of their episcopal ordination as successors in the presiding ministry of a local church (*Church and Justification*, §216). When appeal is made to the Holy Spirit's guidance, especially in preserving solemn definitions from error, this is a criterion of the church's witness to the word of God, especially by councils, and is not contrary to the gratuity of salvation given in justification. The teaching ministry as such serves the communication of doctrinal truth, not the mediation of forgiveness of sins and justifying grace (*Church and Justification*, §219).[72]

---

70. The description of doctrinal development rests on Vatican II's *Dei Verbum*, no. 8, especially the second paragraph.

71. Similarly, *Apostolicity*, §§426–28. For example, "While magisterial teaching issued as fully obligating represent for Catholics a necessary word of the church in given situations, history shows that they are not the church's last word" (§427).

72. The Catholic account is here denying the relevance of the Lutheran appeal

Considerations moving forward

Here, deeply rooted convictions meet and oppose each other.
For defusing their church-dividing character, one could start by
probing the place in Catholic doctrine of the power of the word
of God to interpret itself—as is held dear by Lutherans.[73] A further step would be to go deeper into the theory and practice of
the Catholic teaching office, in its role as an instrument of God
for defending and interpreting divine revelation amid ever-new
historical contexts of church life and worship. A parallel concern would be to probe afresh the relation of charisms and the
central offices of the church.[74]

5. THE PARISH CONGREGATION OR DIOCESE AS "CHURCH" IN THE FULL SENSE

*Lutherans and Roman Catholics have expressed differences regard-
ing where the "fullness" of "church" in a "synchronic, here-and-now
sense," is realized, discerned, and identified, whether in the local parish (congregation) or in the local church led by its bishop (diocese)*
(Church and Justification, *§84;* Church as Koinonia of Salvation, *chs. II–III).*

Lutherans hold the church to be present in all its essential elements in a congregation of believers in which the gospel word
is preached and the sacraments administered, both by right-
fully called ministers (CA 7).

---

in §213 to justification doctrine as the ground of the asserted reservation
regarding binding doctrine.

73. This could involve examining the *Apostolicity* study, part 4, on the biblical
canon, and the Pontifical Biblical Commission's documents on interpreting the
Bible in the church (1993) and on the inspiration and truth of the Bible (2014).

74. This restates with some additions the movement in via indicated in
Communio Sanctorum, §68.

Catholics hold that a particular church of Christ is truly present where a portion of God's people is entrusted to a bishop with his clergy, to be formed into one by the Holy Spirit and by eucharistic celebrations (*Church and Justification*, §92; *LG* 26–27 and *CD* 11).[75] Bishops, according to *Lumen Gentium*, have essential ecclesiological significance, since they are "the visible principle and foundation of unity in their own particular churches. . . . In and from these particular churches there exists the one unique Catholic Church" (*LG* 23). The sacrament of episcopal ordination gives access both to the bishop's ministry of preaching, presiding in worship, and governing and to his membership in the universal episcopal college, which is an important locus of apostolic succession. In the college, each bishop represents his church and brings it into the communion of the whole church, with the communion of the churches expressing itself as communion among the bishops between themselves and the bishop of Rome. In the local diocesan church, the bishop is the living connector between the universal college in communion with the bishop of Rome and the church in a particular place (*Apostolicity*, §§243–44).[76]

Nonetheless, Catholics do not deny the significance of the parish, because it is the site of the major events of proclamation, instruction, baptismal initiation, confession and reconciliation, confirmation, marriage, and eucharistic worship. It is the parish that is most familiar to Catholics as the place where the church is experienced (*Church and Justification*, §93).[77] Vatican II

---

75. The formulation follows closely *Christus Dominus* 11, where the term *portion* was deliberately preferred to *part*, because a portion contains all the essential features of the whole, which is not the case with a part.

76. Concluding a section, "The Episcopal Office," *Apostolicity*, §§240–44.

77. However, the major event of ordination to Catholic pastoral ministry regularly occurs not in the parish church but in the diocesan cathedral, to better express the bishop's role and the sacramental incorporation of the ordinand into the diocesan corps of deacons or the presbyterate of priests.

statements point to the importance of the parish, where the church shows itself visibly when believers are gathered by the proclaimed gospel and share in the eucharist at the same table (*LG* 26; *Church as Koinonia of Salvation*, ch. I). Catholics, together with Lutherans, have affirmed that Christians share in the *koinonia* of salvation most immediately in the worshiping community gathered around the baptismal font, the pulpit, and the eucharistic table (*Church as Koinonia of Salvation*, §36).

While Lutherans do not induct individuals into the episcopal office by sacramental ordination and do not have a worldwide episcopal college as a part of their church structure, they do value regional, national, and worldwide realizations of the ecclesial community. Congregations manifest communion with each other by agreement in the apostolic faith, sharing the same sacraments, and mutual recognition of ministry. Lutheran congregations have formed significant connections with one another in different ways through organization into dioceses (e.g., synods, districts), national church bodies, and The Lutheran World Federation (*Church and Justification*, §§86–90; *Communio Sanctorum*, §52; *Church as Koinonia of Salvation*, ch. III).

Furthermore, the polity of the constituted Lutheran churches of the world is not "congregational" (as CA 7–8 might lead outsiders to think), but is always regional or synodical. Historically, this follows from the Lutheran reform being introduced officially into principalities or into domains of autonomous cities of the Holy Roman Empire. Options for the Reformation did not occur at the level of parish congregations. Through visitations, an *episkope* began to be exercised over the congregations of the region. This practice of visitation continues to be a Lutheran concern. A 2009 study by the United Evangelical Lutheran Church of Germany (VELKD), for example, concluded that visitation is "at the heart" of the task of *episkope* and "a witness to the catholicity and apostolicity of the Church of Jesus Christ."[78]

Today in The Lutheran World Federation "member churches" are distinct from several "recognized congregations," which find themselves alone in countries having no other Lutheran congregations or national structure. The former comprise the "communion of churches" while the latter are recognized as Lutheran in light of their doctrinal commitments and self-understanding, but they have no role in the governance or structure of the communion, since they are not considered to be "churches."[79]

The Apostolicity of the Church explains the Lutheran "differentiation of the ministry" as resting on the congregational pastors' need of such *episkope* or oversight because of their fallibility regarding correct gospel preaching and sacramental adminis-tration (§263). This, one must admit, is a point of Lutheran–Catholic agreement! The text goes on to declare that the internal differentiation of the one ministry, between congregational and supra-congregational tasks, is *necessary*—whatever form the latter may take or whatever title be used for it (§265).

---

78. *Visitation* elaborated this point: "This oversight is not a secondary concern in the church; it belongs to its essence. In the Nicene Creed, for example, we confess our common faith 'in the one holy, catholic and apostolic church.' This faith is demonstrated in visitation. Because we thus recognise that the church exists in local congregations but must be understood as a worldwide community ('catholicity'). And in each visitation we have to answer the question whether we are still teaching and living 'in line with the origins' (namely, according to the 'apostolic' gospel)" (Mareile Lasogga and Udo Hahn, eds., *Visitation: A Study by the Theological Committee of the VELKD*, Bishops Conference of the VELKD [2009], 10). With the intention of strengthening the LWF communion, the VELKD shared an English translation of this study with all member churches.

79. See the LWF Constitution V, which limits membership in this "communion of churches" to churches. Isolated congregations exceptionally can "affiliate" with the work of the LWF but cannot be members.

Considerations moving forward

In the Lutheran–Catholic difference over the realization of "church" in the full sense, different views of the bishop affect what is said regarding the significance of the parish congregation assembled for worship and of the reality and importance of regional expressions of ecclesial community and oversight. However, since Catholics affirm the value of the parish and since Lutheran church polity includes a necessary ministry of regional oversight, our actual church structures are in fact similar in important ways.[80]

B. Ministry

Remaining differences on the ministry are especially diverse, and some appear to be particularly intractable. In addition to the controversies dating from Reformation times, new difficulties on this topic have emerged during the last half century. Nevertheless, newly identified theological frameworks offer perspectives allowing for nuanced, graduated, and differentiated evaluations that provide an alternative to sharp either/or assessments of ministry. A correlation of ecumenical progress made on the church with issues of ministry is an especially urgent task, since such a correlation could support a qualified but immediate mutual recognition of ministry in such a way that a partial recognition of ministry would correlate with the real but imperfect communion of churches.

---

80. See below, in the Ministry section, the treatment of the Lutheran and Catholic differences connected both with the Vatican II doctrine on episcopal ordination and collegiality and with the ongoing Lutheran reflection on episcopal ministry.

1. THE MINISTRY AND CONTINUITY OF APOSTOLICITY

Together, Catholics and Lutherans have articulated complex under-standings of apostolicity, with multiple dimensions, which allow each tradition to recognize apostolic elements in the other, includ-ing in the other's ministry. But an important asymmetry remains: Lutherans recognize the apostolic character of Roman Catholic min-istry, but Catholics do not so recognize Lutheran ministry.[81]

According to Catholic teaching, in Lutheran churches the sac-ramental sign of ordination is not fully present because those who ordain are not themselves in recognized apostolic suc-cession. "Therefore the Second Vatican Council speaks of a *defectus sacramenti ordinis* (*UR* 22) in these churches" (*Apostolic-ity*, §283). This perception of a *defectus*, when understood as "lack" or "absence," clearly stands in the way of recognition of Lutheran ordained ministry.[82]

A number of recent dialogue reports, however, explore alter-natives to such strong interpretations of *defectus*. The rec-ommendation of the U.S. document *The Church as Koinonia of Salvation*, for example, is that "Catholic judgment on the authenticity of Lutheran ministry need not be of an all-or-nothing nature" (§107). In this view, "*defectus*" is to be understood as "defect" or "deficiency" rather than "lack,"

---

81. The Lutheran position was sketched in the *Malta Report*: "Lutherans never denied the existence of the office of the ministry in the Roman Catholic Church. . . . Lutheran confessional writings emphasize the churchly character of the Roman Catholic communion. Also, changes in the understanding and practice of the Roman Catholic ministerial office, especially the stronger emphasis on the *ministerium verbi*, have largely removed the reasons for the reformers' criticism" (§64).

82. The English translation on the Vatican website is currently "the absence of sacrament of Orders" (*UR* 22; http://www.vatican.va/archive/hist_councils /ii_vatican_council/documents/vat-ii_decree_19641121_unitatis-redintegratio _en.htm, accessed June 18, 2015); for "lack" in official English translations see *The Church as Koinonia of Salvation*, §167.

consistent with "the sort of real but imperfect recognition of ministries" proposed by this dialogue (§108).[83] The report then reasons backward from the affirmation of the Decree on Ecumenism, which had said, "Our separated brothers also celebrate many sacred actions of the Christian religion. These most certainly can truly engender a life of grace in ways that vary according to the condition of each church or community, and must be held capable of giving access to that communion in which is salvation" (*UR* 3). The U.S. dialogue continues:

> If the actions of Lutheran pastors can be described by Catholics as "sacred actions" that "can truly engender a life of grace," if communities served by such ministers give "access to that communion in which is salvation," and if "the salvation-granting presence of the Lord" is to be found at a eucharist at which a Lutheran pastor presides, then Lutheran churches cannot be said simply to lack the ministry given to the church by Christ and the Spirit. In acknowledging the imperfect *koinonia* between our communities and the access to grace through the ministries of these communities, we also acknowledge a real though imperfect *koinonia* between our ministries. (*The Church as Koinonia of Salvation*, §107)

In *The Apostolicity of the Church*, emphasizing especially recognition of correct doctrine, the international dialogue reaches a similar conclusion (§§292–93; see also *Justification in the Life of the Church*, §291–95, which appropriates this argument).

---

83. The document cites Walter Cardinal Kasper: "On material grounds [aus der Sachlogik], and not merely on the basis of the word usage of the Council, it becomes clear that defectus ordinis does not signify a complete absence, but rather a deficiency [Mangel] in the full form of the office." ("Die apostolische Sukzession als ökumenisches Problem," *Lehrverurteilungen-kirchentrennend?* III, 345; quoted in *The Church as Koinonia of Salvation*, §108.)

At this point the questions of recognition of apostolic ministry clearly are inseparable from the questions of eucharist. *The Church as Koinonia of Salvation* cites a letter from then Joseph Cardinal Ratzinger to the German Lutheran bishop Johannes Hanselmann showing the close relation: "I count among the most important results of the ecumenical dialogues the insight that the issue of the eucharist cannot be narrowed to the problem of 'validity.' Even a theology oriented to the concept of succession, such as that which holds in the Catholic and in the Orthodox church, should in no way deny the saving presence of the Lord (*Heilschaffende Gegenwart des Herrn*) in a Lutheran [*evangelische*] Lord's Supper."[84]

This tenth round of the U.S. dialogue was in explicit continuity with their predecessors in the fourth round. While characterizing the statement as a "tentative conclusion" for the Catholic participants, *The Church as Koinonia of Salvation* cited the 1981 conclusion: "We ask the authorities of the Roman Catholic Church whether the ecumenical urgency flowing from Christ's will for unity may not dictate that the Roman Catholic Church recognize the validity of the Lutheran Ministry and, correspondingly, the presence of the body and blood of Christ in the Eucharistic celebrations of the Lutheran churches" (*Eucharist and Ministry*, §54; cited, with attention to the supporting studies in *The Church as Koinonia of Salvation*, §124. The same appeal had been made already in the *Malta Report*, §63).

---

84. "Briefwechsel von Landesbischop Johannes Hanselmann und Joseph Kardinal Ratzinger über das Communio-Schreiben der Römischen Glaubenskongregation," Una Sancta 48 (1993), 348; quoted in *The Church as Koinonia of Salvation*, §107. Translation here from Cardinal Joseph Ratzinger, *Pilgrim Fellowship of Faith: The Church as Communion*, eds. Stephan Otto Horn and Vinzenz Pfnür (San Francisco: Ignatius, 2005), 248. The full text of the 1993 letters of Bishop Hanselmann and the then Cardinal Ratzinger is given on pp. 242–52.

Considerations moving forward

Thus, the correlation between this important and long-divisive ministerial topic and the recognition of real but imperfect ecclesial communion between Lutherans and Catholics provides a model and a basis for real but partial recognition of ministries. Such a recognition would capture the "on the way" quality of relations between Catholic and Lutheran communities of faith and would be the single most significant step concerning ministry that would move Lutherans and Catholics toward greater ecclesial communion.

2. THE RELATIONSHIP BETWEEN ORDAINED MINISTRY AND THE PRIESTHOOD OF THE BAPTIZED

Catholics and Lutherans have sometimes characterized one another's position on the priesthood of the baptized in ways that imply important differences on this point. Catholics sometimes assume that Lutheran ministry is a delegation to exercise the ministry of the universal priesthood in such a way that there is no difference between the office of ministry and the priesthood of the baptized. Lutherans sometimes speak of the priesthood of the baptized as a rediscovery by the Reformation.

Lutherans and Catholics agree that "all the baptized who believe in Christ share in the priesthood of Christ" (*Apostolicity*, §273). Moreover, they have said together that the priesthood of the baptized, sometimes called the "common priesthood," and the special, ordained ministry do not compete with one another (*Apostolicity*, §275). Both office holders and the universal priesthood are essential to the church as is evident in Luther's assertion, "Where you see such offices or office holders, there you may know for a certainty that the holy Christian people must be there. For the Church cannot exist without such bishops, pastors, preachers, and priests.

And again, they cannot exist without the church; they must be together" (*On the Councils and the Churches*, WA 50:641, 16–19 [*LW* 41:164]).

Catholics express the difference between the common and the hierarchical priesthood by saying that they differ "essentially and not only in degree" from one another (*Lumen Gentium*, §10). The two cannot be seen as two points on a continuum, with the ordained priest being more intensively a priest or a "higher" priest than a baptized person or two priesthoods being considered as two degrees of priesthood. This difference in essence also means that this ministry is not derived from the congregation, that this ministry is not simply an enhancement of the common priesthood, and that the ordained minister is not a Christian to a greater degree (*Ministry*, §20, note 23; *Apostolicity*, §238). The two priesthoods are two different kinds of participation in the priesthood of Christ even though they are interrelated.

Like Catholics, Lutherans believe that in baptism individuals are initiated into the priesthood of Christ and thus into the mission of the whole church. All the baptized are called to participate in, and share responsibility for, worship (*leitourgia*), witness (*martyria*), and service (*diaconia*) (Lund Statement, §36), and there is a dimension of "mutual accountability" among all members of the church (§52).[85] However, only the ordained exercise the public office of ministry, an office conferred not by baptism but by ordination. The Augsburg

---

85. "In the church there is no absolute distinction between the directed and the directing, between the teaching and the taught, between those who decide and those who are the objects of decision. All members of the church, lay and ordained, exercising different ministries, stand under the word of God; all are fallible sinners, but all are baptized and anointed by the Spirit. Mutual accountability binds together ordained ministers and other baptized believers. Episcopal ministry is exercised within the communion of charisms and within the total interplay of ministries in the church" (§51).

Confession states that no one should teach publicly in the church or administer the sacraments without a proper public call (CA XIV). This call is part of a process of authorization and a requirement for ordination and never simply a delegation to act on behalf of a congregation. All the baptized are priests, but not all are given the office of ministry. Furthermore, the authority of the office is not derived from such authorization. The source of the authority of office is the office itself and the word of God that created the office.

The traditional Catholic assumption about Lutherans does not account for the asymmetry between the Catholic distinction between the common and ministerial priesthoods, on the one hand, and the Lutheran distinction between the universal priesthood and office, on the other hand. In other words, Lutherans do not consider the ministerial office to be a priesthood distinct from the universal priesthood, but do see it, insofar as it is an office, as something that is not either contained in or derived from the universal priesthood. Lutherans, for their part, need to recognize the Catholic emphasis on the priesthood and the ministry of the whole people of God.

Considerations moving forward

Both traditions in recent years have stressed the common priesthood as they seek to call forth the gifts of all the baptized. Both traditions then face the common challenge of articulating clearly and persuasively the proper relationship between ordained ministry and the common priesthood. Thus, both Catholics and Lutherans need to clarify further the relation between the universal or common priesthood of all the baptized and the special ministry conferred by ordination (*Apostolicity*, §167). Differences between the traditions on this point are not church-dividing. On the contrary, here is an example of a nondivisive difference in which particular insights and struggles of Catholics and Lutherans can help each another toward their shared goal.

3. SACRAMENTALITY OF ORDINATION

Catholics consider ordination to be one of seven sacraments, while Lutherans do not call it a sacrament.

Lutherans use the word *sacrament* more restrictively than do Catholics, usually only identifying baptism and the Lord's supper as sacraments. On the Lutheran side this difference is not considered to be divisive. As early as 1981, the international dialogue report cited the Apology of the Augsburg Confession[86] to note that in principle a sacramental understanding of the ministry is not rejected" for Lutherans (*Ministry*, §33). The German dialogue document *Communio Sanctorum* appeals to the same paragraph in the Apology, which "weighs" the designation of ordination as sacrament, and concludes, "The Lutheran Church has thus neither conclusively defined its own understanding of the sacraments nor condemned other understandings. It therefore does not consider the use of the term *sacrament* in a more far-reaching sense by other churches to be church-dividing" (§83; see Apology 13:17). Similarly, in the Swedish-Finnish dialogue, the Lutherans said that their view of ministry "includes a sacramental aspect," although the term *sacrament* is not typically used (*Justification in the Life of the Church*, §279).

Crucially, for Lutherans as for Catholics, ordination, like baptism, is considered unrepeatable. The *Malta Report* saw in this once-for-life character a sort of equivalence in practice to the

---

86. After explicating differences with "the opponents," the Apology continues, "But if ordination is understood with reference to the ministry of the Word, we have no objection to calling ordination a sacrament. For the ministry of the Word has the command of God and has magnificent promises like Romans 1[:16]" (Apology XIII.11, *BC* 220).

Catholic view of a "priestly character," as understood in contemporary theology. (See The *Malta Report*, §60.)

For Catholics, the German study *The Condemnations of the Reformation Era: Do They Still Divide?* suggests that, if progress could be
made toward recognition of apostolic succession, it should be considered "whether the wide degree of agreement about essential
components of the act of ordination does not justify recognition of
the sacramentality of the ordination carried out in the Protestant
churches."[87] *The Apostolicity of the Church* described the common
practice in ordinations: "The Christian is called and commissioned,
by prayer and the laying of hands, for the ministry of public preaching of the gospel in word and sacrament. That prayer is a plea for
the Holy Spirit and the Spirit's gifts, made in the certainty that
it will be heard. Christ himself acts in the human rite of ordination, promising and giving the ordinand the Holy Spirit for his or
her ministry" (§277). As *The Ministry in the Church* had declared,
"Wherever it is taught that through the act of ordination the
Holy Spirit gives grace strengthening the ordained person for
the life-time ministry of word and sacrament, it must be asked
whether differences which previously divided the churches on
this question have not been overcome" (§33).

Considerations moving forward

Thus, it would seem possible to assert officially that teaching
about the sacramentality of ordination is not church-dividing.

4. WHO CAN BE ORDAINED?

*A disagreement of growing prominence between Lutherans and Cath-
olics concerns who can be ordained. Many Lutheran churches ordain*

---

87. Karl Lehmann and Wolfhart Pannenberg, eds., *The Condemnations of the
Reformation Era: Do They Still Divide?* (Minneapolis: Fortress Press, 1990), 152.

women, while the Catholic Church considers itself not authorized to ordain women. In recent years, this difference has complicated issues of mutual recognition of ministry.

Agreeing that ministry is not the personal possession of the minister or to be claimed as a right, both Catholics and Lutherans believe that the church helps to call forth, nourish, test, and confirm the vocations of those who are to be ordained. Both Catholics and Lutherans have changed over time in their practices concerning who can be ordained.

Most Lutheran member churches of the LWF hold themselves free under the gospel to ordain women. They see in this practice "a renewed understanding of the biblical witness" which reflects "the nature of the church as a sign of our reconciliation and unity in Christ through baptism across the divides of ethnicity, social status and gender" (Lund Statement, §40). At the same time, "it can be said that in general the Lutheran churches which have introduced the ordination of women do not intend a change of either the dogmatic understanding or the exercise of the ministerial office" (*Ministry*, §25). Significantly, churches in the LWF that do ordain women and those that do not have remained in communion with one another.

The Catholic Church does not consider itself as authorized to ordain women.[88] Nevertheless, in *The Ministry in the Church* the international dialogue commission affirmed that the Catholic Church "is able to strive for a consensus on the nature and significance of the ministry without the different conceptions of the persons to be ordained fundamentally endangering such a consensus and its practical consequences for the growing unity of the church" (§25).

---

88. John Paul II reiterated this position in the 1994 Apostolic Letter *Ordinatio Sacerdotalis*, §2, 4.

Considerations moving forward

Much ecumenical work is needed to resolve how a mutual recognition of ministry can advance given this asymmetry between
Lutheran and Catholic views on who can be ordained. A number of ecumenical dialogues have found it possible to make
many common affirmations regarding ministry without resolving this issue. Nevertheless, at this moment these issues constitute a significant difference in theology and practice between
the two traditions, and it has not been determined how church-
dividing these differences might be or how the questions for
further discussion might best be articulated.

5. Distinction between bishops and priests/ministers

*Another issue that has become more problematic for Lutherans and
Catholics in recent decades arises from new Catholic teaching from
the Second Vatican Council. The teaching of* Lumen Gentium *that
episcopal consecration confers the fullness of ordination (LG 21,
27) introduces the ecumenical question whether this way of distinguishing between priests and bishops creates a new dividing issue
between Lutherans and Catholics.* The Apostolicity of the Church
*observes, "When Vatican II emphasizes the episcopate as the basic
form of church ministry, it gives prominence to a difference from
the Lutheran understanding of ministry, which is fully realized in
the public service of word and sacrament in the local community"
(Apostolicity, §115).*

Before the Second Vatican Council, the relation between
priests and bishops was for Catholics a more open question.
While traditionally the distinction between presbyters and
bishops was located in the powers proper to each, because a
bishop could ordain and confirm while a priest could not, it
was also clear that practices had embraced considerable diversity and change over time. Historical research, for example,

shows some exceptional circumstances when some abbots were given jurisdiction to ordain their monks in the medieval period (*The Church as Koinonia of Salvation*, §169). When considered across the broad sweep of history, then, no absolute borderline has existed between a priest and a bishop as regards the powers of ordination.

Vatican II expanded the theology of the episcopate by identifying it as the fullness of the sacrament of order, by emphasizing that episcopal consecration is also an ordination and not just additional jurisdiction, and by situating the episcopacy within the episcopal college. The teaching of Vatican II that the bishop possesses the fullness of the Sacrament of Order[89] amounts to saying that there is a "continuum" within sacramental ordination, but this should not be interpreted as a *gradus honorum* as if a bishop accumulates lower orders before achieving the fullness of orders. Thus, the present ordering within the *Pontificale Romanum* (1990) begins with the rite for a bishop and presents the three orders in a descending order, indicating that the other two orders, deacons and priests, participate in the one sacrament of order whose fullness resides in the bishop. The bishop possesses the fullness of the Sacrament of Order not because he was ordained first as deacon and priest, but because episcopal ordination invests him with that fullness. That fullness includes both the bishop's identity as priest and his responsibility for *diaconia*.

Furthermore, the sacramentality of episcopal consecration indicates that a bishop is ordained to the threefold office including the governing office of pastoral leadership, the sanctifying office of priesthood, and the prophetic office of preaching and

---

89. The singular, Sacrament of Order, is used here even though English often uses the plural, Sacrament of Orders, since the Latin is *sacramentum ordinis*, singular.

teaching. The episcopal powers associated with this threefold office derive from the Sacrament of Order and not from jurisdictional canonical mission. Finally, the episcopacy is inherently collegial, episcopal ordination incorporating the new bishop into the worldwide college of bishops.[90] As *Lumen Gentium* states, "The order of bishops is the successor to the college of the apostles in their role as teachers and pastors, and in it the apostolic college is perpetuated" (*LG* 22). *The Apostolicity of the Church* concludes from this teaching, "For Vatican II the episcopate thus becomes the basic form of ordained ministry and the point of departure for the theological interpretation of church ministry" (§241).

Current Lutheran reflection on *episkope* and those who exercise this ministry reflects both important internal diversity in the world communion and a consciousness of the importance of ecumenical engagement on this important subject. It is striking that the LWF celebrated its 60th anniversary in 2007 with its Council's unanimous approval of the *Episcopal Ministry within the Apostolicity of the Church* (known as the Lund Statement). While such an action cannot bind Lutheran churches, nevertheless, in the words of LWF General Secretary Ishmael Noko, "Speaking in unison on this important subject both required and demonstrated matured depth in the ecclesial identity of our communion and growing strength in relations among our member churches" ("Preface"). Calling for "ecumenical awareness" at every step, the Lund Statement

---

90. The Council of Trent prepared for this paradigm of episcopal ministry. *The Apostolicity of the Church* comments that even though it "took as central the category of priesthood . . . it enlarged the concept so as to include pastoral tasks." Furthermore, "By assigning the position of pre-eminence to the bishop, Canon 6 represents a basic change of direction in the understanding of the Sacrament of Order, moving away from the Eucharistic body toward the ecclesial body of Christ and its members" (§§231–32). This expansion of the theology of ministry beyond an exclusively eucharistic paradigm allows for greater affinity with Lutheran theologies of ministry.

concludes that as "Lutheran churches continue to develop their theology of ministry in the face of the many challenges posed within their respective contexts," they need to "develop a broader common understanding of how episcopal ministry points to the diaconal dimensions of the apostolic tradition and also of how the personal, collegial and communal dimensions of episkopé take shape in practice" (§61, using the threefold language for dimensions of ministry made central by *BEM* and used frequently in subsequent dialogues). Thus, Lutheran practice, while continuing to maintain characteristic emphases on the oneness of ordained office and the possibility of variety in structural expression in response to contextual demands, nevertheless has clearly become a more open partner with Catholics in understanding the distinctiveness of episcopal ministry.

The U.S. dialogue statement, *The Church as Koinonia of Salvation*, suggests a possible way of understanding the distinction between a bishop and a presbyter/pastor. It describes the difference in terms of the *koinonia* over which each has oversight and thus in terms of "their service to different levels of ecclesiality." The "normative complementarity" and mutual dependence that exist between the "face-to-face eucharistic assembly" and the "primary regional community" parallel a similar complementarity and interdependence between local and regional ministry. This perspective highlights the specific emphases of Lutherans and Catholics with their strengths and challenges. At the same time, it emphasizes also "the profound similarities" between the "distinct but inseparable offices" in their mutual interdependence: both bishops and presbyters are ordained to serve word, sacrament, and the pastoral life of the church" (*The Church as Koinonia of Salvation*, §82–94).[91]

---

91. Titular bishops, who are members of the episcopal college and either serve the universal church (most often in a Roman dicastery) or assist their ordinary as auxiliary bishops in larger dioceses, contribute to the communion of the

Considerations moving forward

At this point in the discussion of ministry, it would be helpful for Catholics to declare the beginning of canon 7 from the Council of Trent, "If anyone says that bishops are not of higher rank than priests, or have no power to confirm and ordain, or that the power they have is common to them and the priests,"[92] as nonapplicable to Lutherans today.

Furthermore, dialogue discussions provide encouragement that agreement between Lutherans and Catholics about the difference between a bishop and a presbyter/pastor is sufficient to determine that the teaching of Vatican II on the fullness of order conferred on a bishop need not be church-dividing. Such an interpretation, however, calls both partners toward growth in understanding of the relation between ministerial identity and the nature of the church as *koinonia*. Catholics, for example, could continue to interpret *Lumen Gentium's* teaching as emphasizing more the bishop's responsibility for *koinonia* than his more extensive episcopal powers. Lutherans can attend to a more robust understanding of the collegial dimension of episcopal ministry in overseeing *koinonia*. Here again, a more explicit correlation between ministry and ecclesiology points a way forward toward a mutual recognition of ministry.

6. Universal ministry and Christian unity

The questions of a universal ministry of the church and the roles of bishop of Rome are among the most longstanding and obvious differences between Lutherans and Catholics.

---

church in their distinctive roles even though they do not represent a particular church in the communion of churches.

92. Council of Trent, Session 23, 15 July 1563. Tanner, 744.

The Apostolicity of the Church notes, "There is no controversy between Lutherans and Catholics concerning the essential relation between each worshipping congregation and the universal church; nor do we differ over this relation being perceptibly represented and mediated in diverse ways. But there is a dispute about what intensity and what structure this relation to the universal church must have for the worshipping congregations and individual to be in accord with their apostolic mission" (§287).

For Lutherans, questions about global structures for unity have an internal dimension. While certainly their own "communion in a worldwide framework is less developed" than for Catholics (*Apostolicity*, §287), it has in recent decades been strengthened in a number of dimensions. Lutherans continue to seek the best institutional expressions for their unity throughout the world, especially through the communion identity of The Lutheran World Federation. In other conversations, Lutherans continue to ask themselves about possible recognition of a ministry of unity for the bishop of Rome.

For Catholics, the bishop of Rome as the successor of Peter is both a member of the worldwide college of bishops and the principle of unity of that college as well as of the multitude of the faithful (*LG* 23).[93] Catholic ecumenical discussions of universal ministry and its role in promoting unity intersect with calls to explore "how the universal ministry of the bishop of

---

93. This was already stated at the First Vatican Council in the Prologue to the definitions on the papacy: "In order that the episcopate itself might be one and undivided and that the whole multitude of believers might be preserved in unity of faith and communion by means of a closely united priesthood, he placed St. Peter at the head of the other apostles and established in him a perpetual principle and visible foundation of this twofold unity." (Vatican I, Session 4, July 18, 1870: First Dogmatic Constitution *Pastor aeternus* on the Church of Christ, DH 3051).

Rome can be reformed to manifest more visibly its subjection to the gospel in service to the *koinonia* of salvation" (§117).

In his 1995 encyclical *Ut unum sint,* John Paul II invited ecumenical dialogue partners to explore with him "the forms in which [the universal] ministry may accomplish a service of love recognized by all concerned." He acknowledged that "the Catholic Church's conviction that in the ministry of the bishop of Rome she has preserved . . . the visible sign and guarantor of unity constitutes a difficulty for most other Christians, whose memory is marked by certain painful recollections." He continued, "To the extent that we are responsible for these, I join my predecessor Paul VI in asking forgiveness." Desiring to "seek—together, of course—the forms in which this ministry may accomplish a service of love recognized by all concerned," he asked, "Could not the real but imperfect communion existing between us persuade Church leaders and their theologians to engage with me in a patient and fraternal dialogue on this subject, a dialogue in which, leaving useless controversies behind, we could listen to one another, keeping before us only the will of Christ for his Church and allowing ourselves to be deeply moved by his plea 'that they may all be one . . . so that the world may believe that you have sent me' (Jn 17:21)?" (*Ut unum sint,* §§88, 95–96).

While the full potential of the invitations in *Ut unum sint* remains to be realized, the topic of the exercise of universal ministry has received repeated attention from Lutherans and Catholics, both before and after the encyclical. As early as the *Malta Report* in 1971, the office of the papacy as a visible sign of the unity of the churches was not excluded insofar as it would be subordinated to the primacy of the gospel by theological reinterpretation and practical restructuring (*The Gospel and the Church,* §66). Its task was envisioned as helping to maintain the universal church in the apostolic truth, as serving the worldwide full communion of churches, and as encouraging local and regional churches in their faith and ministry (cf. Luke 22:32).

In the United States, Round V, *Papal Primacy and the Universal Church* (1974), examined a number of attitudes toward the ministry of the pope, including ways in which this ministry could "serve to promote or preserve the oneness of the church by symbolizing unity and by facilitating communication, mutual assistance or correction, and collaboration in the church's mission" and also ways in which it historically has provided "a major obstacle to Christian unity" (§4). Round X, *The Church as Koinonia of Salvation* (2004), urged the question, "If the interdependence of assembly and ordained ministry is typical of the structure of the church at the local, regional, and national level, then why should such an interdependence not also be found at the universal level?" (§118). For Lutherans, taking this question seriously would involve asking themselves "whether the worldwide koinonia of the church calls for a worldwide minister of unity and what form such a ministry might take to be truly evangelical" (§120).

In Germany, Catholics and Lutherans have been able to say together that "a universal ministry serving the unity and truth of the church corresponds to the essence and the task of the church, which is realized on the local, regional, and universal level. It is appropriate to the nature of the church. This ministry represents all of Christendom and has a pastoral duty to all particular churches" (*Communio Sanctorum*, §195).

In Sweden and Finland, *Justification in the Life of the Church* (2010), seeking to contribute to "the continuation of the talks on the ministry of Peter as a service to wholeness and unity," concluded, "The reformers were willing to accept the pope on condition that he was willing to submit to the gospel. The same conditions are repeated in the Catholic–Lutheran dialogue, which has opened for the possibility of a ministry of Peter as a visible sign of the church as a whole, on the condition that this ministry is subordinate to the primacy of the gospel. This would however mean a change or an adaptation of the current structure of the papacy. A possible task for the Lutheran–Catholic dialogue would be to define further what the gospel requires in this context" (§328).

Considerations moving forward

Issues of papal ministry, especially in regard to authority and jurisdiction, raise questions that have no promise of imminent resolution. Discussion between Lutherans and Catholics about what "in service to the gospel" would mean for the exercise of papal primacy are still in their early stages. Nevertheless, even the fact that these discussions are no longer at the first stage is significant. Commitment exists both internationally and regionally to pursue these issues with greater concreteness and specificity.

Moreover, other dimensions of a universal ministry have a special timeliness in our cultural moment. Manifest changes in the exercise of papal leadership offer the possibility of renewed discussions of this ministry. In a time of growing global awareness and instant communication across many lines of division, the bishop of Rome bears witness to the Christian message in the wider world through evangelization, interfaith relations, and promotion of social justice and care for creation. A question still to be fully explored is how he may bear this witness on behalf of both Lutherans and Catholics.

C. Eucharist

In matters concerning the eucharist, the dialogues have discovered and set forth convincingly that Lutherans and Catholics do share common views. The *Declaration* has articulated six significant agreements in the area of eucharist. Lutheran–Roman Catholic dialogues in recent decades have also dealt with differences related to the Lord's supper that have not yet been fully reconciled. However, the dialogues also have demonstrated that many perceived disagreements are mitigated by clarification and understanding of one another's terminology. In certain cases, each side has grown in appreciation for the positions espoused by the other side.

1. EUCHARIST AS SACRIFICE

*Historically, Lutherans and Catholics have had disagreements about how the terminology of "sacrifice" should be applied to the eucharist. In recent ecumenical consensus, both sides have affirmed that it is appropriate to speak of a "sacrifice of praise" in connection with the eucharist (*The Eucharist, §37). *Still, the Catholic–Lutheran dialogue group for the Swedish-Finnish church (2010) observes: "From a Reformation perspective, it is however unusual to describe the church as involved in the sacrifice of Christ" (*Justification in the Life of the Church, §230). *Thus, some Lutherans continue to regard the language of "sacrifice" found in Catholic theology and the Catholic eucharistic rite to be a potential stumbling block to unity.*[94]

---

94. In the *Roman Missal*, 3rd ed. (2010), the priest says: "Pray, brothers and sisters, that my sacrifice and yours may be acceptable to God, the almighty Father," and the people respond: "May the Lord accept the sacrifice of your hands for the praise and glory of his name for our good and the good of his holy church." The *General Instruction of the Roman Missal* (#95) asserts: "In the celebration of the Mass the faithful form a holy people, a people of God's own possession and a royal Priesthood, so that they may give thanks to God and offer the unblemished sacrificial Victim not only by means of the hands of the Priest but also together with him and so that they may learn to offer their very selves."

In his 1520 treatise *Babylonian Captivity of the Church*, a text that is formative for many Lutheran pastors and other Lutheran leaders, Luther used strong language to argue against the terminology of "sacrifice" as he understood it to be employed by many of his contemporaries (*LW* 36:35). For the 16th-century reformers, the "diminution in practice of congregational communion was regarded as scandalous, and the primary blame for this was placed on the idea of the Mass as a propitiatory sacrifice. It was thought that this idea allowed for a view which made unnecessary the reception in faith of Eucharistic grace and attributed an autonomous sacrificial power to the priest" (*The Eucharist*, §59).

However, as the 1978 U.S. dialogue statement, *The Eucharist*, explains: "All those who celebrate the Eucharist in remembrance of him are incorporated in Christ's life, passion, death, and resurrection. . . . In receiving in faith, they are taken as his body into the reconciling sacrifice which equips them for self-giving (Romans 12:1) and enables them 'through Jesus Christ' to offer 'spiritual sacrifices' in service to the world (1 Peter 2:5)" (§36).

Considerations moving forward

Ecumenical conversations have shown that many of the perceived disagreements are mitigated by clarification and understanding of what is intended by the Catholic language of "the sacrifice of the Mass." Furthermore, both research into the historical background of the Reformation polemic and considerations of new developments in both churches have proved especially helpful. In *The Eucharist*, the members of the Joint Commission assert, "We can thankfully record a growing convergence on many questions which have until now been difficulties in our discussions. . . . [A]ccording to the Catholic doctrine the sacrifice of the Mass is the making present of the sacrifice of the cross. It is not a repetition of this sacrifice and adds nothing to its saving significance. When thus understood, the sacrifice of the Mass is an affirmation and not a questioning of the uniqueness and full value of Christ's sacrifice on the cross" (§61). Thus, we encourage increased attention to the instruction and formation of clergy, as well as increased catechesis of the laity, regarding the teachings of their own traditions, and greater knowledge and sympathetic understanding of one another's traditions.

2. MODE OF EUCHARISTIC PRESENCE

"Roman Catholic and Lutheran Christians together confess the real and true presence of the Lord in the Eucharist" (The Eucharist, §48). *However, there are differences in their theological statements and terminology about the mode of presence.*

Catholics widely use the term *transubstantiation*, employed by Thomas Aquinas and the Council of Trent (DS 1642), to describe the ontological transformation of the original substances or central realities of the eucharistic bread and wine into the substance or reality of the divinized body and blood of Christ. In its 1978 document, the international Joint Commission stated, "In order to confess the *reality* of the Eucharistic presence without reserve the Roman Catholic Church teaches that 'Christ whole and entire' becomes present through the transformation of the whole substance of the bread and the wine into the substance of the body and blood of Christ while the empirically accessible appearances of bread and wine (*accidentia*) continue to exist unchanged" (*The Eucharist*, §49, quoting Council of Trent, DS 1641).

However, members of the international Joint Commission (1978) have suggested that this difference in understanding the mode of presence need not be church-dividing "if both sides were to profess the reality of the presence in a sufficiently clear and unambiguous manner and, further, if the mystery-character of the Eucharist and the eucharistic presence of the Lord were to be affirmed."[95] They have further recommended that Lutherans should not therefore regard the Catholic doctrine of transubstantiation as a rationalistic attempt to explain the mystery of the presence of Christ in the sacrament but rather understand this doctrine "as an emphatic affirmation of the presence of Christ's body and blood in the sacrament."[96] They also recommended that "Catholics, on the other hand, should recognize that a clear and unambiguous affirmation of the real presence of Christ—as is indeed given by the Lutheran side—can no longer form the subject of an *anathema sit* ['let that person be anathema'].[97]

Considerations moving forward

Building on Lutheran and Catholic affirmations of eucharistic presence, and our shared concerns to confess the mysterious but real presence of the risen Christ giving himself to the recipient in the eucharist, we encourage our increased attention to the instruction and formation of clergy, as well as increased catechesis of the laity, regarding Lutheran and Catholic teachings about the mystery of Christ's presence in the eucharist. Clergy and other church leaders are urged to study one another's traditions carefully in order to gain a

---

95. "Supplementary Studies: The Presence of Christ in the Eucharist," in *The Eucharist*, §§62–63.

96. "Supplementary Studies: The Presence of Christ in the Eucharist," in *The Eucharist*, §63, quoting *The Eucharist as Sacrifice* II. 2c, 195. See above, the historical note in Agreement No. 4. In fact, the Catholic doctrine is not defined as "transubstantiation" but is a "conversio" ("conversion," "change"). The Council of Trent calls the term *transubstantiation* "fitting" (DS 1642 and 1652).

97. "Supplementary Studies: The Presence of Christ in the Eucharist," in *The Eucharist*, §63, quoting *The Eucharist as Sacrifice* II. 2c, 195.

sympathetic understanding of these traditions and to instruct others as accurately as possible so that each side may avoid mischaracterizations of the other's beliefs and practices.

3. RESERVATION OF THE ELEMENTS/EUCHARISTIC DEVOTION

Traditionally, Lutherans and Catholics have had differing views and practices regarding the reservation, use, and disposition of the eucharistic elements after the conclusion of the liturgical celebration. Both Lutherans and Catholics reserve the elements to commune the sick, the homebound, and others unable to be present at the eucharistic service.[98] *Other practices, however, have often been the subject of disagreements. Many Lutherans have taken exception to Catholic practices of adoration of Christ in the eucharistic elements outside the eucharistic celebration.*

As the report of the U.S. dialogue *The Eucharist* explains:

> According to Catholic doctrine, the Lord grants his Eucharistic presence even beyond the sacramental celebration, for as long as the species of bread and wine remain. The faithful are accordingly invited to "give to this holy sacrament in veneration the worship of *latria*, which is due to the true God." Lutherans have not infrequently taken exception to certain of the forms of Eucharistic piety connected with this conviction. They are regarded as inadmissibly separated from the Eucharistic meal. On the other hand, Catholic sensibilities are offended by the casual way in which the elements remaining after communion are treated sometimes on the Lutheran side. (§§53–54, quoting Council of Trent DS 1643)

---

98. Cf. *The Use of the Means of Grace: A Statement on the Practice of Word and Sacrament*, adopted for Guidance and Practice by the Evangelical Lutheran Church in America (1997), Application 48A, p. 49.

In the encyclical *Ecclesia de Eucharistia* of April 17, 2003, Pope John Paul II affirms as highly important the worship of Christ present under the eucharistic species outside of Mass, which pastors must encourage (no. 25). The same recommendation is echoed in Pope Benedict XVI's post-synodal exhortation, *Sacramentum Caritatis* (Feb. 22, 2007), in §§66–69. Critical comments came from Lutherans seeing this as troublesome in view of the relatively recent origin of the practice and of its practice in only the Latin Rite.[99] However, after three decades of ambiguity, the practice is increasing again among Catholics, both young and old.[100]

It may be helpful to note that Lutheran concerns about the adoration of Christ in the eucharistic elements outside of the eucharistic celebration have their roots in Reformation-era polemics—written at a time when people received communion rarely and viewing the elevated host was seen as a powerful form of contact with Christ as a sort of substitute for receiving communion. In the current situation where Lutherans and Catholics now are encouraged to commune frequently, and parishes regularly make communion available, the concern about the eucharistic adoration supplanting reception of communion is less justifiable.

The Catholic concern about Lutheran disposition of the eucharistic elements is addressed by words of Luther and instructions given to Lutheran churches. Luther had instructed the Lutheran pastor Simon Wolferinus not to mix leftover consecrated eucharistic elements with consecrated ones. Luther

---

99. George Lindbeck, in a symposium on John Paul II's encyclical in *Pro Ecclesia* 12 (2003), 405–14; also Richard L. Jeske, "*Sacramentum Caritatis*: A response," *Ecumenical Trends* (September 2007), 12.

100. Prayer before the tabernacle came up so strongly, especially from the audience, at the 2008 Quebec International Symposium on Eucharistic Theology that the Laval theology faculty devoted to it a whole issue of the pastoral journal *Lumen Vitae*, that is, vol. 64 (2009), no. 3.

told him to "do what we do here [i.e., in Wittenberg], namely to eat and drink the remains of the Sacrament with the communicants so that it is not necessary to raise the scandalous and dangerous questions about when the action of the Sacrament ends" (WA, Briefweschel X: 348f.). Ministers in the Evangelical Lutheran Church in America are instructed: "Any food that remains is best consumed by presiding and assisting ministers and by others present following the service" (*Use of the Means of Grace*, Application 47b, p. 48).

The 2010 Swedish-Finnish Catholic–Lutheran dialogue statement, *Justification in the Life of the Church*, notes: "It has . . . become increasingly usual in the Church of Sweden either to keep the Eucharistic elements in a special place or to consume them completely" (§235). The U.S. dialogue recommends that "for Lutherans the best means should be adopted of showing respect due to the elements that have served for the celebration of the Eucharist" (§55).

Considerations moving forward

Both traditions assert the need for reverence due to the eucharistic elements following the conclusion of the eucharistic service. Further reflection and dialogue is necessary on the purpose of the reservation of the eucharistic elements after a liturgy is concluded, on the continuing presence of Christ in the elements, and on the propriety of adoration directed to Christ in the reserved eucharistic elements, for in this area an important, though not church-dividing, difference remains at this time.

4. EUCHARISTIC FELLOWSHIP

In our churches, there are different regulations regarding the invitation of nonmembers to receive communion. Most Lutheran congregations invite baptized believers to receive at the table. In the Catholic

Church, normally only those in full communion with the Catholic Church are invited to receive the sacrament.

Lutherans and Catholics generally concede that the eucharists we now celebrate are imperfect signs of the church's unity, because not all baptized Christians can share in them. Thus, the catholicity of the church is not present in its fullness because of this separation of baptized Christians at the table of the Lord. Baptism unites them, but this division keeps them, and their faith and life, at a distance from each other. Consequently, catholicity is not operative in the Catholic Church in a full manner (*UR* 4). Furthermore, this separation at the eucharistic table means that our unity in Christ is not manifested to the world.

This division has lamentable effects in the lives of individuals, including the pain suffered in Lutheran–Catholic marriages, when one spouse cannot receive communion in the other's congregation. Our churches have grave need of development in our pastoral practice to justify occasional eucharistic hospitality. Based on the present *Ecumenical Directory* and looking toward the general good, especially for those in Lutheran–Catholic marriages, Catholic communities might increase the opportunities for Catholics and Lutherans to receive communion together. Already local Catholic bishops, given the principles stated in §§129–31 of the Pontifical Council for Promoting Christian Unity's *Directory for the Application of the Principles and Norms for Ecumenism*, can develop their considerations of "grave and pressing need" (§130) to receive the eucharist. This should be done in light of (a) the full possibilities of the principles stated in the *Directory* and (b) the spiritual good of Lutherans well-disposed to receive the eucharist, especially for those in Catholic–Lutheran marriages who attend church regularly, those who make retreats in Catholic retreat houses and similar venues, those gathered for ecumenical meetings, and so forth.

Considerations moving forward

Neither of our churches has agreed on a definitive position about what intermediate sacramental steps, if any, might be taken to help lead to reconciliation and full communion among separated Christian communities. The possibility of occasional admission of members of our churches to eucharistic communion with the other side *(communicatio in sacris)* could be offered more clearly and regulated more compassionately.

V. Next Steps on the Way

Together with the *Joint Declaration on the Doctrine of Justification*, the 32 agreements in this *Declaration on the Way: Church, Ministry, and Eucharist* are instances of the imperfect but real and growing unity of Catholics and Lutherans. With the authoritative teaching of the *JDDJ*, guidance from dialogue documents like *From Conflict to Communion*, and the many efforts at all levels to deepen the relations between our two traditions, reception of *Declaration on the Way: Church, Ministry, and Eucharist* can become an occasion to renew our commitment to continue together on the way to full communion.

We, therefore, recommend that The Lutheran World Federation and the Pontifical Council for Promoting Christian Unity together receive, affirm, and create a process to implement consequences of the 32 "Statements of Agreement on Church, Ministry, and Eucharist" in section 2 of *Declaration on the Way: Church, Ministry, and Eucharist*. Receiving these agreements culled from international and regional dialogues recognizes that

there are no longer church-dividing differences with respect to these statements and emphasizes their cumulative importance. Thus, such recognition is itself a further step on the way.

Moreover, reception of these agreements invites The Lutheran World Federation and the Catholic Church to implement practices that would express and advance this growing communion between them.

- Creation of a process and a timetable for addressing remaining issues on church, ministry, and eucharist is clearly an important step forward.

- The expansion of opportunities for Catholics and Lutherans to receive Holy Communion together would be a significant sign of the path toward unity already traveled and a pledge to continue together on the journey toward full communion.

- Lutherans and Catholics will continue to advance on the path toward unity by addressing the moral issues that are often deemed to be church dividing in the same spirit of mutual respect and commitment to unity characterized by their work on issues of justification, church, ministry, and eucharist.

In addition to these initiatives, full reception of these 32 agreements at local and regional levels invites a number of pastoral responses specific to particular contexts that would include the deepening of many common activities well established. In many places substantial steps have already been taken. In each context Lutherans and Catholics will have to find the most appropriate ways forward to continue their journey toward full communion. Some recommendations to continue or to initiate these efforts for fostering unity include:

Prayer

- For Lutherans and Catholics to let their yearly Week of Prayer for Christian Unity prayer time serve as an impetus to pray together and meet more regularly during 2016 and 2017.

- For local Catholic and Lutheran clergy to gather regularly for common prayer and study. Our agreements on ministry indicate that Catholic priests and Lutheran ministers are in real, if imperfect, communion with each other. This communion might manifest itself in regular prayer together, in study of the ecumenical documents listed above, and in regular spiritual retreats.

Education

- For local Catholic and Lutheran religious educators to develop together materials that inform their students about the most important aspects of our communities. This might include study of key elements from our histories and from the major documents mentioned earlier with ideas for their local implementation.

- For local congregations of Catholics and Lutherans to study the Bible together—especially the New Testament—as individuals and in small groups.

- For members of Lutheran and Catholic parishes and other local Christian communities to learn more about each other by spending time during 2016 studying texts such as *JDDJ, From Conflict to Communion,* and *Declaration on the Way* in preparation for the commemoration of the Reformation in 2017.

- For Lutheran and Catholic seminaries to provide opportunities for all their students to learn about the progress in Catholic–Lutheran relations.

Collaboration

- For local Catholic and Lutheran bishops to establish a permanent Lutheran–Catholic working group for their region. A local group would (a) seek out the best practical ways to collaborate and (b) recommend to church leaders new or renewed collaborative action(s) and provide for continuity in efforts for other ministries.

- For Catholics and Lutherans to work together to care for those with spiritual, emotional, and physical needs in their community. Many already work together for social justice. We believe that our collaboration must be rooted in prayerful discernment of what God would have us do, perhaps beyond our current ministries.

- For local Lutheran and Catholic bishops to work together with each other and with clergy and laity to encourage collaboration in prayer, study, and service. This collaboration by the bishops could include identifying local leaders for various ecumenical projects.

- For local Catholic and Lutheran parishes to enter into covenants with one another. This might include promises to pray for each other at each Sunday liturgy, regular gatherings for prayer and study, and common sponsorship of local ministries.

All of this flows from Jesus' prayer for his disciples after the last supper, "That they may all be one" (John 17:21).